BÔ YIN RÂ

THE BOOK
ON
LIFE BEYOND

Do not be discouraged ever, as
you struggle along the way. It is
the greatest possible detriment to
your progress, the worst obstacle
you can create to block your path.
—PARAMANANDA

For more information about Bô Yin Râ
and which book titles are available, visit
The Kober Press web site at
|www.kober.com.

BÔ YIN RÂ
(J. A. SCHNEIDERFRANKEN)

THE BOOK
ON
LIFE BEYOND

TRANSLATED FROM THE GERMAN
BY B.A. REICHENBACH

BERKELEY, CALIFORNIA

English translation © 1978 by B. A. Reichenbach

Eric Strauss, Publisher & Editor

For permission to quote or excerpt, write to:

THE KOBER PRESS
2534 Chilton Way
Berkeley, California 94704
email: koberpress@mindspring.com

This book is a translation from the German of the second edition of *Das Buch vom Jenseits*, published in 1929 by Kober'sche Verlags-buchhandlung, Basel-Leipzig. The copyright to the German original is held by Kober Verlag AG, Bern, Switzerland.

Printed in the United States of America

Library of Congress Control Number: 78-051633

International Standard Book Number: 0-915034-11-5

Typesetting and design by Irene Imfeld, Berkeley, CA

Book cover after a design by Bô Yin Râ

Second edition 2002

CONTENTS

INTRODUCTION

THE FOLLOWING THREE chapters are to give you an idea—to the extent one can by means of words—of what you will encounter once your present life has ebbed away and you will be set free from this domain of physical perception.

Like a traveler's guide book, which can tell you much about a country of this earth that you have never seen, the present volume, too, was written to provide you with the most important facts concerning that—to you still unknown—world in which you one day shall awaken, capable of feeling and experience, no matter whether you at this time can believe that such a future life exists, or not.

This book shall, at the same time, clear your mind of many errors, by which your thoughts are still misled when you reflect on those who once were dear to you in life on earth, but whom you had to bury.

Anguish-ridden faith and rampant superstition, both of old and modern times, have brought forth such a host of mental phantoms regarding the "beyond" that now there is great need to sift through this confusion, so that baseless fictions may no longer cloud your mind.

The only human beings who truly have authentic things to say concerning life after the material body's death are the few exceptions who, from lucid personal experience, already know that other life, which needs no earthly body. In their external mortal lives, however, these exceptions also still participate in every joy and sorrow of this present life, like you.

As one of those who are already fully conscious in that life beyond, I shall relate what can be told in words; for we can feel the longing of this age, which rightly may expect that factual experience of spiritual life, though it have reached the consciousness of but a few, ought not to be kept secret knowledge any longer.

May you benefit from what I have to tell you!

May my words be able to awaken your awareness of your inmost self, so that you will discover—within your proper consciousness —that kind of inner certitude which best will guard you from falling prey to either sterile skepticism or to a blind belief in every sort of fantasy created by confused or overly excited mortal minds.

Within yourself alone you are to find the touchstone whereby you always shall be able to determine how much truth and how much fiction the various ideas contain that mortal man created for himself, from his beginnings, to give himself the strength he needed to endure the dark and awesome mystery which opened up before his eyes each time he stood beside a lifeless human form.

WHETHER YOU BELIEVE or not what I shall have to say will not make any difference, because the facts that I describe do not depend on your opinion or approval. Besides, I do not set forth creeds or dogmas that would require your assent. Instead, I show you a dimension of reality that, at this time, you cannot get to know except by way of *concepts,* which human language can convey.

Soon enough you, too, will find yourself alive in this dimension of reality. Then you will *know* what place is to be yours within it.

Authentic testimony concerning life beyond was given man in every age, through all of human history. Yet in the past such testimony fell prey to minds without authority and calling, and felt no scruples in corrupting it to serve their own designs. Therefore you need help today if you would learn to disentangle things that must be sorted out; for else you might reject not only the chimeras of benighted dreamers, but also the accounts of those who brought authentic knowledge: insights no perceptive soul would want to treat with scorn.

If you would fully grasp the substance of this book you should attempt to put aside all preconceived ideas. But seek to listen now and then if there is any echo stirring in your heart;

for from within yourself, if you but learn to hear, you shall receive the answers to those questions that this book will yet leave open, since you are meant to find such answers for yourself.

THIS BOOK IS NOT INTENDED to recruit adherents for some new hypothesis of metaphysics or philosophy; nor is it meant to found a new kind of "religion." Its only purpose is to offer you authentic knowledge concerning the objective *spiritual*—not intellectual—*experience* that was the source and origin of all the ancient great religions which, in their time and place, were born out of the Spirit that is God's.

Thus, to have the contents of these pages come to life within the reader's heart he need not give up the religious faith that he regards as sacred. On the contrary, what I convey will rather deepen and confirm the faith of those for whom time-honored rites and dogmas are still a genuine necessity of daily life. And thus it may revive their faith in their beliefs.

For those, however, who long since have outgrown the bonds of organized religion, my words will once more clear the path to realms of spiritual life, that will forever be the goal of human being's deepest longing; even though the concepts and beliefs that used to guide their forebears could not grant them the fulfillment they had ardently desired, in a form consistent with their own conceptual capacities.

CHAPTER ONE

THE ART OF DYING

I T IS MOST LIKELY your opinion that the act of dying is not so much an "art" as a neces-sity, bitter and inexorable, and that one learns it rather quickly, without much need for preparation.

Millions think like you; and countless mortals die each day, leaving behind their physical organism, who never learned the art of dying.

To very many death comes unexpectedly, "as a thief in the night," while others see him as a specter they abhor. To some he comes as a long-awaited, merciful redeemer from their agonies, while others even seek him of their own free will, in the belief that death will solve their every problem and release them from all pains of soul and mind.

Very seldom death meets someone who has learned the art of dying.

To know this art and master it, you first will have to learn, in days of health and energy, what the event of "death" is in reality, and also what it means to "die."

You have to *practice* dying, as it were, while you are still in full possession of your health and powers, so that you will know how to die, and profit from the art of dying, even though your death should face you unexpectedly.

Dying is not quite so easy as many seem to think. Nor is it, on the other hand, particularly difficult if one has learned it in days of strength and vigor.

Every art requires practice, and without practicing one cannot ever learn the art of dying.

All this notwithstanding, you one day shall have to experience "death," whether you have learned to die or not.

Most people are afraid of dying because they have no clear conception of what is taking place.

And those who claim that they are not afraid are rather like small children who venture on the ocean in a little boat, but do not know the dangers of the sea.

You, however, shall be like a helmsman who understands the winds and tides, and also knows about the land he can expect to find when he arrives upon the ocean's other shore.

You are to learn how you yourself can set the course and guide your well-prepared, sea-worthy vessel.

To DIE MEANS: to be forced to give up all control of one's material body, its organs and its senses, and to relinquish this control forever, irreversibly, when owing to physical reasons the organism is no longer able to sustain its life.

Something very similar takes place each time you fall asleep; then, however, you give up sleep only part of your control over your body and its senses, and merely for a certain time, while through death you lose control of it completely and forever.

Nature herself, as you can see, is teaching you the rudiments of dying.

Similarly, when you faint, or when your consciousness is artificially suppressed you can foretaste what dying is.

However, in these cases you only get to know the first part of the actual experience; unless, that is, your *spiritual* senses already are sufficiently developed to allow you to awaken on the "other side" of life, where to your great surprise you then will find yourself alive *without* any physical body.

But if you never had such an experience you may at least gain some idea of conscious life without your present body by learning from your dreams; to be sure, your life "beyond" is something other than mere dreaming.

It is only to assist your comprehension that I remind you of your dreams.

For, just as in your dreams you are not only conscious—capable of feeling, thought, and action—but also have a body that you use at will, even though your physical organism is resting fast asleep, so also will you find yourself in bodily existence—conscious, feeling, thinking, acting—when you are able, on the other side of life, to use your *spiritual* senses, and thus discover that you are *alive*; whether this be only for brief periods or, in the event of death, without return.

There is, however, one essential difference. For in your dreams you merely face the ever changing phantoms called forth by the plastic force of your imagination; but what appears to be their tangible existence is only due to countless physical and psychic causes. By contrast, in order to awaken in the objectively existing world of Spirit—no matter in which of its domains this shall occur—you have to leave the world of dreams behind, just as you must leave it in order to awaken in the world of physical perception.

ONCE YOU HAVE SURMOUNTED the sphere of dreams, then only can you enter the realm of *spiritual* reality. You will not find it difficult to tell this realm apart from even your most vivid, life-like dreams; for, owing to your spiritual senses, you here possess such clarity of self-awareness that even the most lucid moments in your present physical existence seem only like a leaden slumber by comparison.

Awake within that realm, you hear and see and feel the very same reality that you perceive in *physical* existence. In the waking state of mortal life you experience this reality as the domain of physical phenomena, or "nature"; then, however, you will be able to perceive its "other side."

That is to say, you then will see those elements and aspects of the realm of final causes that used to be "invisible" to your bodily senses; and, at the same time, everything that only mortal senses can perceive—the whole of what is now your "real" world—has suddenly become thin air and disappeared.

Although not many people may actually have known such an experience—or may know it even now—their numbers are much greater than one would suspect; for most of them instinctively decide to keep their knowledge secret; either from the fear that others might repay their confidence with doubt or even ridicule, or from concern that such experience of spiritual reality, which they see as a special grace, might in future be denied them if they failed to keep it to themselves.

WHILE THOSE WHO THUS may consciously experience this reality within themselves are yet unable to enter any of the Spirit's higher realms, they nonetheless have truly reached "the other side." Even so, they still are far from being able to enter the *interior* of the *land* they have discovered, nor can they hope to scale its *towering peaks*.

This innermost domain is open, during life on earth, to only those few living mortals who were entrusted—here, on the physical side of what is the domain of final causes—with man's eternal heritage of spiritual knowledge and experience. Born to this end, they then become the high priests, the masters of the Spirit's timeless work; and they alone choose also their successors, who are likewise born as such.

The proven knowledge we have gained of life "beyond," through long, direct experience, is given to you in this book.

Every day and every hour we see human beings by the thousands make their crossing to the "other shore," from which they never will return, and yet we cannot help them; for in their time on earth they had not learned the art of dying. And so they reach the other side confused and unprepared, cast ashore like shipwrecked victims of a sudden storm.

Aimlessly they err about in what for them is still a new form of existence, and so they fail to recognize and cannot grasp the helping hands that would assist and guide them.

Still incapable of judging what they see, they have no way of telling whether that which they encounter means to harm or help them; and they recoil in fright if someone who could offer guidance would approach them.

And so they stray alone, ever anxious to keep near the "shore," which they believe still links them with the physical dimension of reality they knew, and which they now have left. All such will in the end discover one or the other of the smaller *phantom realms*, a sphere that corresponds to the ideas and notions they had formed in life on earth, and which now satisfies their hopes and expectations. These phantom worlds, to one of which they now will find themselves attracted, as though by a magnetic force, comprise the *lowest* spheres in the domain of spiritual reality, which lies beyond the grasp of *physical* perception.

And here, deluded by the life in such a phantom world, they are convinced that they have found their "heaven." In this belief they grow still more confirmed since everyone they meet here is likewise certain that he is in heaven.

The fate of those who are entrapped in such domains of self-imposed illusion is sealed for endless ages.

Very seldom, and only with the greatest difficulty, can we rescue one who in this manner lost his way, and lead him out again of the deceptive bliss of his imagined heaven.

But since we want you to avoid this fate, and as eternal love directs us to instruct you, we here shall teach you now the art of dying as one ought to know it.

THE VERY ESSENCE OF this art consists in being ready, at any moment of one's earthly life—in the midst of busiest activity and planning for the future, in perfect health and at the peak of physical vitality—to cross the threshold of the other life forever, without all hope of coming back; and, furthermore, to do this willingly, in joyful, confident serenity.

The task is to attain a certain state of mind, a conscious inner attitude.

Although not everyone may find it easy to attain this state of mind, one nonetheless should not forget that in it lies the key if one would rightly learn the art of dying.

PEOPLE WHO ARE SO attached to their possessions in this present life that they feel they cannot do without them, or those who are unable to conceive of any situation in which all aims of earthly life become entirely irrelevant—such people will likely never learn the art of dying.

And yet, the gift of living here on earth not only wisely, but in true and lasting happiness, is granted in the highest form to none so much as those who can create that state of inner readiness at will, at any given moment.

For such a person knows that none of those whom he would have to leave behind—neither those he loved most dearly, nor any being still depending wholly on his care—could, in all eternity, be separated from his presence, unless he were himself to seek this separation and to effect it through his will.

He also knows that he will still be *here,* present at this selfsame place within the universe; indeed, still closer to all those he loves than he could ever be in mortal form.

Again he knows that, having died, he certainly will not at once be changed into a godlike being, nor be "omnipotent" in matters of this world, but that he, nonetheless, will be enabled to give far more effective help to all who need his care than he could ever do in life on earth.

A person who will practice the art of dying in this way thus knows that he will henceforth find it easy to bid this present life farewell—when his time to leave it permanently shall have come—even though his death should face him unexpectedly.

As to the physical event of dying, the reader should remember that medical research has long since recognized, through careful observation, that "death" as such, while sometimes agonizing for observers, is in itself not painful to the dying; for what the latter suffers are but the pains of his respective illness, which he will only feel, however, so long as he has not yet died.

What we are to discuss here is not that, however, but rather how a person's consciousness survives the act of dying.

ALTHOUGH A DYING PERSON may still be fully conscious to the very end, a kind of slumber will come over him the moment when the *spiritual* organism begins to free itself from its connection with the mortal form to which it had been joined until this time. From this slumber the person will awaken, to regain his proper consciousness, only after the event of death already lies behind him.

At the moment of this reawakening, which may occur a few seconds or minutes after physical death can be externally established, the person finds himself already on the *other* side of absolute Reality, and in his *spiritual* organism. This organism will from now on be his only means of gaining individual experience, given that he now lives on the spiritual side of what is absolute Reality. This Reality, the realm of final causes, brings every form of being, all phenomena, into existence—both in the physical as in the spiritual domain—depending in each case upon the manner of *perception* through which this absolute Reality is sensed and apprehended.

Before his death, the individual's perception was determined by the faculties and senses of his physical organism. Now, however, this manner of perception has been superseded by another kind, one that normally he did not know before. But while there has occurred a change in his perceptive *faculties*, his actual *perspective*—whereby he shapes whatever he perceives—remains still what it was.

To be sure, it never would occur to him that he is "dead"; for, after all, he still is fully conscious of his own existence, of his will, and his perceptive faculties; even though he may not yet have recognized that all of his perceptions are now due only to his *spiritual* organs.

Nor does he find himself devoid of shape, without a body; given that his former physical appearance was merely an approximate reflection of his timeless spiritual organism. Although the latter's form and structure are in fact created by man's proper *timeless* will, he is unaware of this within his physical, his purely mental consciousness. Now, however, he is able to perceive his spiritual organism, even though he does not recognize as yet that it is something other than his mortal form.

pain

Any pain a dying person may be suffering before the end will instantly have vanished as he awakens on the other side; in the same way as all pain sensations disappear when the organ causing them is made insensible by the appropriate anaesthetic. Here, similarly, the physical body, which alone had been the source of any pain the person may have suffered, has now been permanently severed from his spiritual organism, which henceforth will be conscious only of its own existence.

HOWEVER, OWING TO extremely fine, invisible, material radiations emanating from the now discarded physical body there still exists a certain *fluidic* bond. This bond, which the spiritual organism feels as well, is the reason why the individual, who has awakened on the other side, can still perceive, by virtue of his spiritual senses, various events occurring near his former body, despite their taking place within the *physical* domain.

For that reason the departed, who now lives on the other side, not only senses the fluidic emanations of those who stand around the mortal form he left behind, but also feels the quality of their emotions, communicated by their touch and words. In addition, he retains, much like someone blind, a fairly accurate conceptual image of external space, from which he has been severed. He only is deceived, however, in thinking that the space perceived is still experienced by material senses.

Such last connections with the *physically* perceived domain of absolute Reality continue to be felt a certain time, even after the body has grown cold. But all the influences sensed this way grow weaker with each passing hour and, after the appearance of the first signs of decay, the faculty for such perceptions ceases altogether.

Those who raise objections to the custom of cremation, or actually believe that it might cause some harm to the departed in his life beyond, should bear in mind that, by the time observed in civilized societies before remains are laid to rest, all sense connections between man's spiritual organism and his former mortal form have long since permanently ended.

But where death is due to fire, organic pain is felt, here as with any other cause of death, up to the moment only when the physically determined consciousness is lost. However, in this case all further contact with the abandoned mortal body is already severed by the time man's consciousness awakens on the other side because of the decay effected by the fire.

Cnc. ANYTHING BUT ENDED, on the other hand, is the departed's full awareness of his own existence —a consciousness that now is wholly owing to his *spiritual* organism and its senses—and his clear perception of the spiritual forms of all those who are physically present. Because their *spiritual* forms, apart from certain limitations inherently connected with the realm of matter, faithfully reflect their *physical* appearance here on earth.

This new condition is often so deceptive to those whose self-awareness during life on earth had never risen much above the level of man's creature consciousness that they quite fail to notice, sometimes for considerable periods after having died, that they no longer occupy a mortal body.

Instead, they think that they have suddenly "recovered," given that the symptoms of their former illness have now completely disappeared.

For the moment their perception is still spellbound by a dreamlike memory of *physical* existence; and while in this condition, the spiritual forms of their grief-stricken relatives—whose objective presence they perceive—become confused with other figures, which are merely the subjective products of their dreams. And now the just departed cannot understand why anyone should mourn for them.

They often then use all their energies attempting to convince those present, who are grieving for them in the physical domain, that there is no cause whatsoever for their sorrow. Yet all their efforts go unnoticed; for those they left behind in physical existence are so distraught by pain and grief that they sense nothing but their own distress.

Only when at last the person recognizes that he has lost his power to make his presence felt among his relatives and friends, and to convince them that their grief is needless folly, only then the now departed suddenly discovers that he no longer occupies a mortal form. And now he finally awakens from the dream that he himself had been creating.

Not until this moment does he truly *learn to see*; for then at last his spiritual eyes have opened and begin to recognize the unfamiliar spiritual side of absolute Reality, whose other aspect of perception, caused by physically determined senses, he has left. This changing of perceptions, however, does not affect the actual "place" which the departed occupies within the structure of the cosmos.

IT IS FROM THIS POINT ON that those who failed to practice the art of dying in their time on earth begin to lose their way among the worlds beyond. For the event of death will of itself not in the least enhance the spiritual organism's faculties of *judgment*, which the person had been able to attain in life on earth.

To be sure, the moment one arrives in life beyond there will be helpers near him willing to *guides* give aid. However, in his present state he fails to recognize them as the guides they are.

Instead, the now deceased, who still is wholly blinded by his former mental prejudices, tends quite resolutely and imbued with self-assurance to reject all their assistance. And so they are prevented from giving any help.

Sometimes, too, the very recognition of having actually attained "eternal" life may fill the new arrival with almost boundless arrogance; and this, of course, will only drive him deeper into folly.

People who were wholly chained to life on earth, and those who worried night and day about concerns and people to whom they now cannot return again in mortal form are gripped at first by agonies of desperation when they begin to comprehend that they shall nevermore be able to return to life on earth. Not until they have lived through this torment, which is a bitter task indeed, will they grow able to perceive their new capacities for being active here on earth. To be sure, these new capacities are purely spiritual in kind.

Those, by contrast, who in this present life were driven by some fixed idea, which they were anxious to see realized, and thus were altogether wrapped up in the thoughts and notions connected with their goals, such will very quickly lose all interest in the existence they have left behind.

The only thing they look for now are ways to implement their fixed ideas within their new environment. And, consequently, they are blind for any other form and possibility of self-experience.

Others again would like to find the "kingdom of heaven" and its bliss, which they were promised and had faithfully believed. But now they are surprised and not a little puzzled because they did not instantly encounter it in life beyond, nor in the form their minds had so attractively envisioned in their days on earth.

All of these, who still are solely occupied both with themselves and with the notions they have carried over from their former life will in the end attain fulfillment of a kind for their respective wishes: by being drawn toward one of the innumerable phantom worlds, to whose existence they had themselves unknowingly contributed already during life on earth.

This transition, too, occurs without the person's changing his location; for all dimensions in the Spirit's realm—and they are infinite in number: from the lowest phantom world to the sublimest realm of light, in which the Spirit forms itself to God—remain forever at the selfsame cosmic place, each one penetrating every other.

Dimensions

The faculty of consciously experiencing a given spiritual dimension, as well as the ability to pass from one dimension to another, requires in each case a change in one's perspective. By virtue of this change the spiritual consciousness is rendered "blind" for

S. Conc.

the phenomena in one particular dimension, and at the same time comes to "see" phenomena existing in another given sphere.

Yet this particular faculty of changing the dimensions of perception cannot simply be acquired by anyone who wishes. None, in fact, can exercise it but the masters representing the eternal self-representation of the Human Being in the Spirit's realm, or their appointed agents, their chosen pupils, to the extent the latters' psycho-physical endowment will permit.

All human individuals, however, even those not of the heritage I here defined, are able to acquaint themselves, at least by way of *empathy*—following the guidelines that we here provide—with the sensations, states of consciousness, and feelings they will have to face the day they leave their mortal forms.

I readily concede that empathy, thus purposely employed, can only bring forth *semblances,* but never lead to any actual experience of one's condition after death.

It is, however, for this very reason that I must insist that one be strictly guided by the expositions of the present book when seeking to evoke the images and feelings essential in this context. For, in the course of physical existence, only very few can ever consciously experience the realm of life beyond; while, through the evocation of images and concepts that *faithfully reflect* Reality, every human being is able to anticipate the various emotions, feelings, and different states of consciousness that he will have to deal with once he has departed from this present life.

One needs repeatedly to practice this experience in advance, so that he may be certain of being able to orient himself the instant when his consciousness is severed from the world of physical perception. And, in particular, that he may clearly recognize what should be sought and what must be avoided.

Only people who have gained the necessary inner certainty already during life on earth will equally be able—after their transition into the domain of spiritual perception—to recognize the helping hands that will be there to meet them, and they alone are capable of grasping them with confidence.

Such a person is prepared, and now can profit from our help.

For in his life on earth he knew to learn the art of dying, and by his trust in our guidance he caused his spiritual discernment to attain the certainty of judgment that he needs.

From all illusions and deceptions such a person will now be safe and well protected.

Past the countless phantom worlds, which mental dreams and speculations generate from misdirected energies of mortal will, we shall directly lead him into the interior of the land that he has entered. And here he will find guidance of profound compassion, which then shall raise him ever nearer to his ultimate perfection.

For, understandably, he did not all at once become a different, a more enlightened, individual for having lost his mortal form.

And so one cannot simply give him, in one instant, whatever he still lacks.

Nothing more than what was his in earthly life is also now his own, and only this he brought with him as his possession.

All things he had been able to "bind on earth" shall also here be *bound* for him, in spiritual life; and that which he had "loosed on earth" shall in the same way now be *loosed* for him in life beyond.

Only step by step can he be guided higher on his long ascent, until one day he shall be able to enter the sublimest realm within the worlds of Spirit: the innermost domain of Light, the realm of infinite and absolute fulfillment.

Spirit

The "ages" he shall need for this ascent depend on the degree of *relative* perfection he had already gained in mortal life; for this perfection manifests the character and elevation of the person's *timeless* will within his proper self-awareness.

"Death"—the passing from the world of physical experience into the realm of spiritual perception—is, without question, an event that one day will occur to you quite irrespective of your wishes. And that which lies in store for you "beyond" is going to be *there,* no matter whether you believe in any afterlife or not.

But, at the same time, you have been given extraordinary power in your *will*. For through your will you are enabled to determine, in the most far-reaching way, all of your future life and fate within the worlds of Spirit: through what you do today by way of preparation.

It is, of course, expected that your conduct in this present life is morally responsible, and always in accord with what is your sublimest inner goal, a goal one reaches only by virtue of unselfish love toward all things that have life.

For, on the other side of physical existence, where all perception is conveyed by spiritual senses, there also are found other worlds, not only the enjoyment of the "blessed."

Indeed, there are domains of agony and desperation, of harrowing remorse; and also spheres where human beings yearn for self-destruction, although their wish can never be fulfilled.

And through such realms must pass all those, without exception, who did not here on earth fulfill the law that calls on every mortal to love his fellow creatures—and *himself*.

LOVE

<u>Love that will fulfill the Spirit's law</u> is anything but sentimental weakness or great emotional exuberance.

Such love is, rather, the profoundest and most energetic *affirmation* both of one's own eternal self and, likewise, all creation. A person animated by such love will consciously <u>perceive</u>, both in himself and every fellow being, <u>only what is good</u>—<u>that which manifests the Spirit's will</u>—even though he may have to defend himself most resolutely against some negative components, which may at the same time express themselves within that very being.

suicides

Those who end their life by their own hand, seeking, for whatever reason, to escape like cowards from the demands and duties of their life on earth <u>commit one of the gravest violations of that very law.</u>

Their attempt to flee is, furthermore, both senseless and in vain. For one who dies by his own hand, instead of finding the escape he sought, <u>will feel his consciousness tormented</u> by a thousand times more painful chains, a state he surely did not seek, but now cannot escape for aeons.

43

Those whom such a person left behind may find a certain consolation in the fact that most suicides are committed at a time the person's consciousness is pathologically disturbed, so that this horrifying act of blind negation is consummated in a frame of mind that one may look on as spontaneous insanity; even though this mental state had long been fostered by the person's irresponsible, continued playing with the *thought* of ending his own life.

Although in such a case both murderer and victim are found within one person, the crime itself was the result of a consuming mental impulse, which the victim had kept feeding with his proper energies, until it overwhelmed and, in the end, destroyed him.

A person who annihilates his physical existence will, therefore, have to bear responsibility less for the act of *murder* than for every misdirected *thought* and *action*, which finally had led him to his insane deed. It is for all such thoughts and actions that now the Spirit's law requires him to make amends.

This can, in most cases, be accomplished only by the person's suffering a *second* physical embodiment, another lifetime as a mortal human creature.

Here is one of the *exceptions* under which "reincarnation" may in fact occur. However, if man's life on earth has run its normal, spiritually provided course any further incarnation has been made impossible once and for all, in that *one* physical embodiment is all the Spirit's law exacts or will allow.

Now, while there is no question that this present life is of profound importance as a means of preparation for your future life beyond, you should not think that, for this reason, you here must lead the trembling life of some guilt-ridden penitent; one of those poor "saints" of little faith who live in constant terror lest their sinful nature rob them of eternal "bliss"; those selfish hearts who for their own part live in fear of every "sin," yet secretly rejoice as they look forward to the prophesied damnation of the "wicked world."

With such an attitude you only would be sure to land in one of the delusive phantom realms, which human folly brings into existence on the other side, without suspecting that they are its *own* creation.

A life devoted to the true fulfillment of your duties, and of compassion for all living things; a life of kindness and integrity; of seeking harmony and order in your mind and will; of striving to refine your tastes and your enjoyments; a life of cheerful faith in that your Spirit's purest longing shall know fulfillment in the end—such a life will always be the best that you can lead in this existence. All the more so if you at the same time seek to learn what in this chapter I have called the *art of dying*.

To be sure, besides the life here outlined there is also a particular and more demanding inner path, which leads to higher realms within the Spirit; this path I have described already in an earlier book. But if you do not live your life according to the principles I mentioned, you will not make much progress on that way.

One who means to enter on that other path must first be free from every burden that might fetter and impede his stride.

Here, a pose of pious melancholy is equally objectionable as the hollow gesture of "renouncing the world."

Not everyone may feel he has the strength to enter on this steeper path, on which a person *Dow* may attain his highest goal—the birth of *God* within his soul—but all at least should know that such a path *exists* and ought to make the effort to prepare themselves to enter it, wherever possible, already in this present life.

Many may still lack the energy and the endurance which this path demands; but all man's spiritual powers, too, grow stronger through their constant use and, here as everywhere, endurance is bestowed on those alone whose heart and soul are dedicated to their goal.

W<small>HATEVER HUMAN BEINGS</small> *think* and *feel* and *do* *Living* on this side of Reality, within the world of physical perception constantly produces its direct effect upon the world *beyond*.

The fruits of every deed that man performs in mortal life remain his very own, lasting far beyond his physical existence, even though his works had merely served his daily needs.

Living So long as what you do is morally responsible, what matters is not *what* you do, but rather *how* you do it.

The lowest menial labor you perform on earth can later bring you unimagined energies within your spiritual existence; provided you fulfill your given duties gladly, with absolute integrity and, to the best of your ability, in such a way as though the very universe depended wholly on the excellence of your performance.

You—and you *alone*—are answerable for yourself, and for the things you do and feel and think.

Although you are not conscious of it at the present, you are yourself the author of your future fate in the domain of spiritual perception; because your every thought and action—no matter what you do on this side of Reality—is constantly affecting what you are *beyond*.

WHAT HERE ON EARTH you call your "fate" is no more than a tiny fragment of one immeasurable whole. And if, perhaps, you curse your fate in this existence, your anger may indeed seem justified and even pardonable—from a human point of view. All the same, you here act rather like a foolish child, who cries for things he cannot yet be given, because they now would only harm him, but which he later shall enjoy abundantly.

You will not truly understand the nature of your earthly fate before you can survey it from a high perspective in the Spirit's world; and then your present views will make you smile if you think back on them.

You then will comprehend that your most weighty arguments, which had misled you to your present judgments, were just so many fallacies; because you thought you could deduce the beauty of the blossom and the sweetness of the fruit from the entanglement of roots your eager hands kept digging from the stony ground.

Only those who can escape the narrow confines that physical perception of necessity imposes on their timeless nature, will more and more begin to sense a glimmer of the all-embracing *Unity* in which their spiritual self is rooted, but which one cannot find or know by means of physical perception.

It was truly not an empty phrase, which long ago a witness used, when all but overwhelmed by what he saw he found the words, "No eye has seen, no ear has heard what God prepared for them that *love* Him."

God | To *love* God, means |, however, to love one's toils and sorrows in this present life; that is to say, so willingly to take them on oneself as though all things that life may bring us were just what we ourselves had sought and wanted.

To *love* God means: to love this earth and every thing upon it—the way it *is,* even though it may conflict with our wishes.

To *love* God means: to love oneself and, for one's own sake, gladly to accept whatever burdens might be given us to bear on our long and arduous ascent that, in the end, will lead us out of error and confusion to *ourselves,* such as we are, eternally, in *God.*

From what you read thus far you also may have gathered how best to honor those you loved in mortal life, but who have passed away. They all are still alive, only now your physical perception will not let you see them.

You now will know how you can still give help to them and, likewise, how you may yourself receive their help if you should ever need it.

It clearly is the wrong approach to hold "séances" in the attempt to conjure up the ghost of one who has departed from this life.

Even presupposing the honesty of all participants, and absolute protection against all kinds of fraud, including its unconscious forms, one still knows far too little of the forces that manifest themselves in such séances; nor is one able to identify the real authors of the various phenomena.

It even makes no difference if one rejects all preconceived ideas and only wishes to establish through "experiments" what truth there might be in the claims of those who do believe in Spiritualism.

The forces that produce all *genuine* phenomena in such séances are very treacherous, capricious, and deceitful; and while they are quite eager to manifest their presence—by means of energies they drain from you—they would not dream of letting you control them as obedient objects for experiments of "psychical research." To be sure, I only speak of genuine phenomena and leave aside the countless possibilities of fraud by mediums and their collaborators.

The genuine phenomena of Spiritualism, which some regard as emanating from a life *beyond,* are in reality, if one excludes all instances of human fraud, nothing more than willful trickery produced by unseen creatures that exist in what is still a largely unknown sphere of *physical* reality.

Given that the few who have objectively *awakened* in the Spirit's world do thus already know and share the life of the departed—even though they also still have mortal bodies in this world of matter—they, too, may be considered here as living on the other side. These few, however, *can* in certain cases use the mentioned occult creatures in the same way as one uses other forms of energy. But none who has awakened in the Spirit's life would ever dream of using them to entertain participants in a séance, or to add an interesting touch to the experiments of some investigator.

Even where one is completely certain of being in the presence of a once incarnate *human* individuality, the likelihood of being duped by these lemurian creatures so far exceeds the probability of any genuine communication that one cannot warn emphatically enough against pursuing any path on which one might encounter *any kind* of spiritualist phenomena.

THE WRITER OF THE PRESENT warning knows every possible variety of such phenomena from thorough and abundant personal experience.

He also knows that occult borderland in which these unseen beings live, as in their proper element. And, if he must, he can make use of these lemurian creatures—which spiritualists assume are "human" spirits—as one employs a horse for riding, or a dog to find a track.

These beings will obediently submit their energies to one who has been granted power in the Spirit, whenever he would use them; nor does he need to hold "séances," or employ a "medium."

For he can enter the domains in which these creatures live as readily as the dimensions of the spirit, in which he likewise is at home and fully conscious.

It is, however, anything but pleasant to come near these beings, and no one who can use them as he wishes shall ever do this needlessly; and he will always have to overcome a sense of inner loathing.

For the purpose of analogy, one might compare these creatures to the jellyfish of southern seas, except that, as a rule, they are beyond the grasp of physical perception. It is with beings of this kind, and with their given energies—which are likewise purely *physical*—that, for the most part, you communicate in fact while you assume to be in touch with a departed "spirit." It is, however, also possible that the phenomena observed are caused by certain energies that you yourself unknowingly possess, and which are rooted in the same dimension as these occult beings. And in that case you would have merely staged a ghostly farce with spooks of your own making.

For your physical and spiritual wellbeing the like unwitting self-delusion is, at any rate, far less pernicious than is all *real* contact with the mentioned creatures. For they will drain your strength like leeches; because they can bring forth the vaunted "wonders" observed in spiritualist séances only with the energy that they have drawn from you.

Not even the most open-minded of investigators who seeks to study these phenomena as merely an observer is protected from the power of the probing tentacles that hold him captive from a sphere he cannot see.

However far he may suppose himself to be "above the situation," it will not save him from becoming a defenseless prey and being drained of his most secret energies; all this without the least suspicion on his part of the abuse to which he is subjected by his medium's hidden parasites, which meanwhile occupy his full attention.

ALL GENUINE CONTACT with those who have already entered into life beyond—the only certain way to reach them—is found within man's soul; and all such contact is of a purely *spiritual* kind.

Your own spiritual organism is the faculty through which you can perceive the influence of the departed.

Every thought that stirs your inmost being, every feeling that imbues your heart and soul is comprehended on the other side, just as here on earth we understand the spoken word.

And also you can in the same way sense the will of those who now live in the spiritual dimension of Reality, provided that your inner faculties are keen enough and you are able to keep silence in your soul. You then will feel their influence as calm and quiet thoughts, or like emotions that seem to touch you from without. And with sufficient practice of your faculties you will not find it difficult to tell such thoughts and feelings from those arising in yourself.

But quite apart from everything that you may consciously perceive, there always is at work a direct, though unconscious interchange between your world and theirs, and in this way you often are the *mediator* of a former mortal in a far truer sense than any "medium" could ever be in a séance, even if a disembodied spirit *wanted* to make use of one.

If you were in the habit of observing the common things that happen in your daily life —soberly, yet with an open eye for the mysterious—you would not seldom find that you were acting in the spirit of a loved one whom you lost, even though you never might have consciously intended to act according to his wishes, were the person still alive.

It might also give you pause that often perfect strangers will do things that one may very much regard as the long-sought fulfillment of a wish that a departed mortal once had ardently pursued, but which he was unable to fulfill in earthly life.

All this is, to be sure, not nearly so exciting as a table that will dance or float about the room, or one whose legs rap cryptic "messages"; let alone the "apparition" of some human shape in which one positively recognizes—hypnotically controlled without suspecting it—

the very voice and features of a former mortal, while in fact one stares at something that is nothing more than a lemurian waxwork effigy.

The outward features have, indeed, been copied from the physical appearance of the former mortal, and even suits or dresses seem to have been resurrected. But through this phantom speaks a creature the sight of which would freeze your blood if you could suddenly perceive it standing near you in its *real* shape, stripped of all disguises.

People who have never witnessed any genuine, let alone spectacular phenomenon in a séance are sure to ask themselves how any reasonable, thinking individual could take such matters seriously. Still, the fact remains that Spiritualism counts millions of professed—and secret—followers and to this day attracts new converts into its unwholesome spell.

The literature on Spiritualism, its theory and practice, already is immense; and though it partly is pure fiction, partly pseudoscience, it still finds eager and excited readers. And as for true "believers," no rank or dignity they might have earned in proper scientific disciplines will here protect them from succumbing to most blatant fraud. Least of all in times of grief, when their consuming passion is to be in touch—once more—with someone whom they deeply loved.

The scholar's mortarboard does not afford sufficient insulation against hypnotic influences from spheres of the occult, and academic gowns, alas, are sheer as gossamer before the probing tentacles of nature's unseen mollusks.

For these reasons, then, a word of warning will here not be superfluous.

THE ENTIRE PHYSICAL AND spiritual cosmos is a unified, organic whole; even though this seamless whole reveals itself in infinitely differentiated *aspects*.

The realm of absolute Reality—the final source and origin behind these differentiated aspects—is, and always has been, open to only very few in every generation.

This ultimate Reality lies not within the grasp of mental speculation, nor can one ever seize it by experiments.

Moreover, there are infinitely varied *levels* of perception—both in the world of physical and in the realm of spiritual experience—and *all* phenomena perceived within a given consciousness, no matter in which realm, present themselves as being the only *true* reality.

Apart from very few exceptions, all living things experiencing existence in the cosmos as a whole can only grasp small fractions of this absolute Reality, and even those they only know, unconsciously transformed, according to their given faculties.

Thus, mortal man's existence in the life *beyond* is equally determined by a change in his perceptive faculties.

It is the same Reality that he continues to experience, but now he does so through his *spiritual* senses. Given that, with the cessation of his body's integrated functions, his physical organs can no longer serve as instruments of self-experience.

Life as such, however, is everywhere, throughout its countless realms, experienced and perceived by means of given *senses*; even though these senses differ fundamentally in kind.

Dying, for the human mortal, is simply an event that of necessity compels him to make conscious use of certain inner senses, which up to then had lain concealed in his *unconscious* life.

These spiritual senses exist, however, already in man's mortal life. Indeed, it is through them alone that he is able to receive impressions—by virtue of his bodily senses—which are inaccessible to any animal, notwithstanding that an animal's perceptive faculties are often infinitely keener than any sense of man.

Only in some few exceptional cases can these senses of man's spiritual organism become active during physical existence. And wherever this is possible it will not happen in a sudden flash of being able to employ one's inner senses, but rather through a process of successive stages, a gradual awakening, which may be gently reinforced, but never willfully produced by artificial methods.

ONE WHO HAS IN FACT awakened—thus gaining
conscious use of his inherent spiritual senses
already during life on earth—will then perceive the various lower realms of absolute Reality, which now he can experience, as though
these realms were interwoven, penetrating
one another. At first he often may have difficulty in deciding whether some experience is
still a part of physical reality, or rather taking
place within the spiritual domain.

Only those few individuals to whom the realm
of final causes, too, is opened from within—
the philosophers' "thing-in-itself"—are ever
able to experience, in addition, the realm of
absolute Reality, the final source of all that is.
This primal realm calls into being all the
worlds that are perceived, both within the
physical and in the spiritual universe.

This absolute Reality is the eternal cause of
life in every form, whether it perceive its self-
existence by means of physical or spiritual
senses.

Considered from the vantage point of absolute
Reality, however, man as such—both in his
spiritual forms and as a mortal creature—is in

truth: *Eternal Life* made manifest as individuated, conscious *self-experience*.

To be sure, it is not easy for this individuated emanation of *Eternal Life*—which, in its physical existence, now finds itself restricted to living only through the senses of an animal— *(Mind)* to comprehend itself as being a distinct and single *individual* and, at the same time, the conscious *focal* point of one immeasurably vast totality: a seamless and inseparable unity, which nonetheless embraces and perceives itself in infinitely varied aspects.

The human mind, confined to semblances of physical experience, has difficulty grasping a concept of an *individuality* that is not separated and divided from the total of some unit.

Viewed from spiritual Reality, however, the concept *individuality* describes the timeless mode of self-representation within the *undivided whole*. Individuality is thus not fragmentation of the whole, but the form in which the Spirit's life reveals and manifests its very being.

It is always all of *Life*, whole and indivisible, that—in each of its innumerable self-representations—experiences its own being, from a particular, unique perspective.

CHAPTER TWO

THE TEMPLE OF ETERNITY AND THE WORLD OF SPIRIT

W<small>E, WHO SHARE</small> this present life with you in mortal form, yet at the same time come to bring you witness of the Spirit, we truly live in a dimension of Reality that differs greatly from the world you know. We too, however, stand as firmly on the ground of this existence as yourself.

Perhaps you think that we are all too far removed from you. But no one could in fact be closer to you than are we.

To be sure, we live not only in your world of *In Spirit* matter, but also in the realm whose substance is pure Spirit. Yet your world, too, is permeated by the realm of Spirit, as a sponge in the sea is permeated with the waters of that sea.

Admittedly, your mortal senses cannot apprehend the realm of *spiritual* substance in which we live in spiritual form.

Before you can experience *spiritual* reality you first must have acquired the faculty for spiritual perception.

And even then you first will have to rise above the many lower worlds in life beyond before you reach the Spirit's inner realm, the source from which the knowledge comes that is conveyed to you this day.

There are many nowadays who seek for us and think that they might be united with us in the realm of Spirit if only they could find our earthly dwellings. But even if they were to meet us in this life they would not have come closer to us in the Spirit.

They would see nothing more than our mortal forms, or hear our mortal voices and, at best, perceive the most external things of our physical existence.

But our *Temple* they could never enter. For that stands on the spiritual side of absolute Reality, not on the slopes of the Himalaya.

There, among the highest mountains of the earth, are only found the dwellings of some of our Brothers from every generation. These are men whose greatness has surpassed all earthly scales and who are living here in absolute seclusion, now as in ages immemorial, that they may keep the sands of time from burying the path that must remain at all times open, if those of us who work in outer life are to perform the task that has become our duty.

For thousands of years our work has been in building our *Temple* in the Spirit's world, and though we labor on it without pause, we never shall complete it altogether.

In every century we add new buttresses and columns, new altars and new chapels according to the Spirit's timeless rhythm and its preordained design, which lies enshrined within the *Temple's* fundaments.

All the temples and altars of the world are mirror images, reflecting aspects of our *Temple of Eternity,* which rises in the Spirit's realm, formed of spiritual substance.

Each of its temporal reflections still reveals—sometimes clearly, sometimes with distortions—what the ancient builders sensed or, if they were true artists, could perceive by way of highest intuition of the design, proportions, and adornments of our sacred *Temple of Eternity*.

This *Temple* is by no means an invention of romantic minds, nor am I speaking here in symbols.

The *Temple of Eternity* is, on the contrary, an objectively existing edifice, erected of the Spirit's substance, and visible as such to spiritual eyes. To beings who perceive the Spirit's world this Temple is no less concrete and real than here on earth to mortal eyes appear the towering cathedrals or temples that were built with stone.

All things encountered in the world of Spirit are experienced as being just as tangible and solid as anything you know in physical existence, through your mortal senses. Indeed, you should be very much mistaken if you thought that in the realm of Spirit one finds only fleeting dreams devoid of shape and substance.

What you perceive in spiritual life are not hallucinations, visions, or other self-created concepts. Nor is it your inherited experience, emerging out of your subconscious in the form of visual "projections."

The things that one perceives by means of spiritual senses effectively exist, in all respects, no less concretely than anything that mortal senses can discern. The spiritually apprehended forms thus correspond completely—even at the very highest level of the Spirit's self-representation—with forms existing in the world of matter. In the Spirit's world, however, these forms are modified according to the laws that govern this domain.

In the world of Spirit, too, you will find lands and seas, majestic canyons and lofty peaks. There, too, are glaciers covered with eternal snow, and gentle, spacious valleys of graceful beauty and profound serenity.

If this sounds too "material"—too "this-worldly"—the reader should consider that, in his present life as well, all his *physical* perceptions are likewise only caused by certain patterns of *impressions*, brought forth by external means. He should further bear in mind that his combined perceptions only represent the physically observable *effects* of certain energies. Thus, all the "names" that we attach to things only signify, strictly speaking, given combinations of individual impressions, which we perceive in fixed, related patterns. For example: the human eye receives the optical impression "white"; the hand notes the impression "cold" while sensing the consistency peculiar to the object touched; and if the mass is stepped on, the ear receives impressions of a crunching sound. And now we signify this complex of impressions—which further may include the observation that the mass will quickly melt, and that its flakes show crystal patterns—by the name of snow.

In order to effect the *physical* perception of this complex of impressions, there are required certain elements, or agents, that can *produce* these sense impressions in the realm of physics. However, to become perceptible to spiritual senses, this given complex of impressions must combine the *spiritual* elements, or agents, required to produce the *spiritual* equivalent of the experience.

On the spiritual side of absolute Reality you also will find "time and space," as well as "cause and effect." Yet our own relationship to these phenomena is very different from what it is in life on earth. *T+S*

What man experiences in the world of Spirit is of the same *reality* as that which he experiences, through his mortal senses, in the world of matter. In timeless life, however, it can only reach his consciousness by way of spiritual faculties.

Nor are the things that one perceives by spiritual senses at all removed, in spatial terms, from physical reality; they merely are no longer subject to the laws that govern physical existence.

In the Spirit's world it is the energy of *will* that causes everything to grow which we require to sustain our spiritual body. And once the fruit has ripened, it is again the energy of will that causes our harvest to be gathered, without toil and labor.

The one thing that is absent from the realm of which I speak are *animals*. Nothing but *NO* the purely formal elements occurring in the animal domain on earth are met with in the Spirit's realm.

But all the "drives," the traits of animal *behavior* that human beings share with other animals, have here completely lost their power over man. Nor is there any trace left of the hostile character that we associate with animal life on earth.

WHAT WE PERCEIVE IN forms that correspond to animal phenomena on earth—and which occur, in perfect beauty, also in the Spirit's world—has nothing any more to do with animal *nature* such as we know it here on earth.

In order to sustain their earthly life, some people will use meat, while others may choose to avoid it. Man's only "food" in timeless life, however, are the equivalents of vegetation, and spiritual *bread* and *wine*.

Needless to say, such bread is not baked in an oven. Nor will such wine cause drunkenness.

However, on the spiritual side of absolute Reality as well, it is through *food* and *drink* that our energy is nourished and restored.

This is also true of a condition very similar to the refreshing sleep that man enjoys when he is physically tired.

But given that, in spiritual life, both food and drink are products of pure *will*, their practical effect is, likewise, no more than the *transformation* of such energy into the substance of the person's spiritual organism.

The spiritual body, unlike its mortal counterpart, need therefore never rid itself of any waste or residue.

All this may well strike certain readers as too "physical," too much like life on earth, to find them able readily to understand it.

What they overlook, however, is that in physical existence, too, all things their senses can perceive are merely *symbols* of events whose real nature lies beyond man's physical perception.

All *Life* in the physical as well as in the spiritual cosmos reveals its self as *motion*.

But all motion of necessity produces *form*.

Since *Life* as such remains forever but itself, all *form* is likewise but the corresponding *symbol* of the selfsame motion, in all dimensions of reality, no matter by what faculties they may be apprehended.

A "kingdom of the spirit" such as many dream of, and which through all of history man always has been taught to fantasize: a realm devoid of substance, forms, and symbols does not exist in any sphere; save in the nebulous domains that certain minds adopt as their "reality."

The "formless Sea of Godhead yet unformed" —a realm that mystics speak of—lies far above all *individuated* life. But if you were to lose yourself within that Sea you would be lost in it forever.

Out of that eternal Sea you once came forth, to form and manifest yourself through your immortal will. Now that this Sea *has* sent you forth, in individuated form, it would forever hurl you back into the universe if you were able to return into its fathomless infinity.

Far from this eternal Sea are the pathetic dreamers who, in their own subconscious, came upon their ancestors' inherited experiences, and then ecstatically *relived* the latter's incapacity—their failure to reach *individuated* light—and thus unwittingly assume that in the like experience they have encountered "God."

LIGHT

THE INMOST WORLD OF LIGHT within the realm of spiritual perception—the world from which we bring you word—exists as the creation, in its formal structure, of all those who are able to experience this collective spiritual realm. Even so, however, every individual remains the sole creator of his own experience

The *will* of every individual is here at one with that of every other, so that each single will remains in perfect unity directed toward the selfsame goal.

For itself, however, every individual will within our common world creates its own experience. Yet this can never interfere with any other will's creation, given that the latter could not be perceived by any other, except through mutually experienced *permeation*.

The world that our will creates for our spiritual perception is, in all respects, as *real* as the world of matter is for mortal man. However, in the realm of Spirit man's will does not encounter any of the obstacles that hinder and confine it in the physical domain.

If we want that something *be*, an act of will suffices for it to *become*.

Being willed, it shall become exactly as we wish, sooner or later, depending on the power of our will.

The creative energies of will alone bring forth what is to have existence in the Spirit's world. On the other hand, when something is no longer meant to be, an act of will again suffices that it vanish, and it will disappear without a trace. In this domain, therefore, the might of will comes very near to man's conception of *omnipotence*.

Only the spiritual world itself cannot be changed or made to vanish any more than could the physical, material universe; given that this inmost world embodies the united will of all who can experience it, and thus is the result of their collective spiritual perception.

THERE ARE, HOWEVER, also other worlds of spiritual perception, worlds of clouded knowledge and misguided will.

These are the worlds of individuals who came to enter life beyond, but had not rid themselves of the confining shackles of their mental phantoms and accustomed chains of thought.

Incapable of rising, in enlightened consciousness, to the sublimest heights of spiritual creation, those who still are blinded in this way create themselves a substitute: a lower kind of phantom world that now reflects whatever concepts had possessed their minds on earth. But the spheres created by such will are fleeting and in the end shall pass away.

For each one here wills something different, and so each will is constantly destroying someone else's world.

Yet even such mere phantom worlds are able to survive for thousands of years, if their existence is sustained by common concepts and beliefs, held and nurtured here on earth for centuries on end, owing to the power of great faith.

Yet all who thus unknowingly create these phantom worlds are constantly at war with their opponents: all those within that realm whose will is striving toward some other goal.

You do not realize how much religious blindness and intolerance, how much hatred between nations, and how much other discord on this planet is merely caused by *repercussions* of the furious defensive battles raging in those phantom worlds that man himself, since ages immemorial, unwittingly created in the lower worlds of spiritual perception.

Because whatever man desires or believes in earnest in this present world brings forth a corresponding world within the lower realms of spiritual perception; a world reflecting man's desires and beliefs. And such a phantom world continues to exist as long as the particular desire or belief, which had produced it, survives on earth and will send other beings into life beyond who likewise are imbued with that desire or belief.

Everything in conflict here on earth is likewise enemy within the world of transient fulfillment, which it unknowingly brought forth in the domains of spiritual perception. And all the battles raging on the other side of life in turn cause hostile repercussions affecting mankind in this present life.

Moreover, both dimensions feed and reinforce each other's hate for their opponents, here and on the other side.

But all these separate domains, these phantom worlds in spiritual existence, are one day doomed to perish, even though their life may seem assured to last for aeons.

One world alone has permanent existence in the realm of spiritual creation: the world originating in the light and knowledge of one eternally united, absolute, collective will. A will no force could ever change, because in it the self-affirming will of every individual reveals itself in absolute identity with the eternal source of *Love,* the final origin of everlasting *Life* itself.

WE, WHO LIVE IN THE ETERNAL, conscious of our own eternity, we harbor no hostility toward any tendency of will or faith, no matter how absurd or reprehensible we might find it.

Nor need we ever guard our spiritual world against a foe. For those who might be our enemies can never reach the spiritual realm in which we live.

No matter what they might have heard about us, no matter what they may suppose or fancy us to be, they never know of what we speak. Nor can they comprehend our witness, so long as they continue to be blind.

Therefore, their hostility toward us would always be directed not against ourselves and our spiritual world, but rather toward a phantom, which they have made of us within their minds.

We, however, see those fleeting worlds, which earthbound mortal will has brought into existence, far below the snow-capped peaks where we have made our timeless home. And we are always present to give help, to anyone who would escape these lower spheres.

However, we can only help one who is pure of will, truthful in his innermost, and willing to demand the highest effort of himself. One who is unshakable in trusting that timeless *Love* will bring him help.

Not many are inspired by such will, and few appear to understand that only when their proper energies have been exhausted have they the right to ask for and receive our help.

Nonetheless, such will exists, such understanding can be found.

Though many a call we hear reveals itself as nothing more than cowardly self-pity, while those who call avoid performing their own share, we also hear the voice of others, who truly did fulfill what man has to accomplish by his proper strength.

Only such can we set free from the domains of earthbound, temporal delusions.

Above all else we can effect within the Spirit we see this liberating guidance as a sacred duty.

For us there is no greater joy than bringing help to those who seek to rise above themselves, to guide them out of darkness to the realms of light.

The path that lies before all others is not the topic of this book.

Suffice it to remark that sooner or later they, too, shall come to realize that their "eternal" world is one of self-produced illusion, not the realm of absolute and permanent fulfillment.

Painful and distressing will be their recognition of this bitter truth. And now their only hope of finding light once more lies at the end of long and thorny roads.

Eternities may come and pass away before their seeking soul may finally approach again the first step on the timeless stairs that lead man to eternal light, to permanent fulfillment of his deepest longing, the source and origin of his eternal self.

THE THINGS I HAVE RELATED here may well strike certain readers as rather strange and far-fetched waking dreams, as "visions" of a "mystic" who lost control of his imagination. And, truly, I am far from holding it against a reader of the present age if he seeks to protect himself from what I say by taking cover behind the like conclusions.

Still, I would advise him, in his own best interest, rather to approach what I convey as the disclosures of a person who has much to tell him about a distant land that he has not yet visited himself.

Other readers might perhaps object to what I say because it differs from the things they may have heard from people who deceived themselves believing they had consciously experienced the world of *spiritual* reality.

As to this claim one needs to know that it, indeed, is possible for someone who is born with the required faculty and underwent a certain schooling, to perceive the lower, most peripheral domains among the many realms of spiritual perception. But no mortal ever can attain the inmost realm of spiritual substance who is not one among the few that have been called to guard man's spiritual heritage on earth.

Even those few guardians to whom this heritage has been entrusted, mortals who are born to undertake this task, always had to first acquire considerable spiritual knowledge as well as practical experience, under venerable guidance, before one found them truly proved and tested, after years of strictest discipline.

The "seers," on the other hand, who have the front to lecture you on their results of "scientific research" pursued on so-called higher planes, as though these spheres were readily amenable to tests and to experiments—are without exception people who, at best, have entered one or the other of the lower realms, which I described as phantom worlds of spiritual perception.

To be sure, such a deluded seer may be reporting in good faith what he had actually perceived in such a realm. Or he may tell of things that some intelligence in life beyond—whose apparition he took for a "master"—had shown him, while entranced in his ecstatic certainty.

LESS OFTEN THAN YOU might suppose has man received authentic witness from what is our world within the Spirit's universe.

The few who did receive such witness in the past, on very rare occasions, would as a rule keep their experiences to themselves, for fear that sacred things might be profaned if they made public what they had been granted.

But there has never been authentic witness from our world conveyed to man except by one of us; for we alone are able to disclose such knowledge.

In the past, these insights were conveyed in private only, and only to a few who labored night and day for inner light and guidance.

Such chary seeding has, however, borne but meager harvests, and so we now make public to the world at large as much as words are able to convey of our knowledge and experience.

In stating what I have to say I do not mean to ask that readers put more faith in me than is accepted custom among intelligent and honest people.

The knowledge that I here convey in words is owing to my *spiritual* nature. Thus, I bear witness to a realm of spiritual existence in which I live with those I call my spiritual *Brothers,* while at the same time I also still take part in earthly life like any other mortal; in all things bound by laws of physical existence and far from seeking to escape its duties.

Nor is what I convey based only on my own experience. Indeed, each word I write reflects alike the knowledge and experience of *all* who are my *Brothers* in the realm of Spirit, united with me in the priesthood that serves within the *Temple of Eternity*.

May the reader of these pages not concern himself unduly with the writer as a person, but rather try to ask himself in quiet whether what I say accords with what he senses in his heart.

At first, the echo of his heart may almost be inaudible; particularly if he is still influenced by thoughts and concepts that derive from any of the lower worlds of spiritual perception.

The higher he has risen above this sphere of influence, the more distinctly he will sense the truth of what I tell him, in his heart.

Those, on the other hand, who still, although unconsciously, collaborate in the delusions of some phantom realm, and thus are spellbound by the repercussions of their self-created mock-reality, all such will hardly feel the urge to break their self-bound fetters.

Also those for whom the "realm of spirit" consists of abstract thought and intellect will probably but smile when they are told about a world of spiritual fulfillment that shows so many elements of physical reality.

The insight that the world of *physical* perception—from the vastest galaxy to the minutest particle of matter—is only molded after patterns found in realms of *spiritual* perception—this is something, it appears, that many find beyond their faculties of comprehension.

And so some readers will feel justified, without examining the matter any further, to relegate my expositions to the realm of fable, or call them wishful thinking.

Reality itself is not, of course, affected in the least by any such mistakes in judgment.

Were it not an ancient superstition that man can apprehend the realm of Spirit by means of logically impeccable deductions, the reality of which I speak here would long ago have been unlocked, so that today it would be known beyond all doubts and questions.

The teachings of the great historical religions, by contrast, come much closer to the truth; for in their wealth of images and symbols much has survived to our day that clearly shows the mark of individuals who truly were awake in life beyond.

A reader who can still interpret the symbolic language of their witness, both in word and art, will not hear unfamiliar things if I declare that man's eternal self shall find no truly everlasting joy but in the inmost, light-begotten world of Spirit with its unending wealth of forms and primal symbols, its infinite potential for fulfillment of man's sublimest form of will.

THOSE, HOWEVER, WHO assume that death will end their conscious life forever when they lose their mortal form need only wait until they die. For then they can themselves revise their fateful error—by their own experience.

They scarcely will think much of what their heart may sense and tell them. And all their mental powers notwithstanding, they fail to see how they themselves obstruct the only way on which they could find real certainty, now while living still on earth.

To be sure, one often finds the best of people on the side of those who, for reasons they think irrefutable, equate the dissolution of man's mortal form with the annihilation of his conscious self. Still, it is most difficult to make them see their error; for they are so deceived by physical reality that they assume the obvious fact of physical mortality is likewise true in a domain that follows altogether different laws.

There is, of course, no question that the human being—as a physically perceptible reality—is destroyed forever when death reclaims his mortal form.

What shall continue to exist is man's eternal, self-formed *will*, such as it revealed itself, before the body's death, by virtue of that body's faculties. And, furthermore, the *consciousness* that recognizes its own self within that individuated will, just as it had known itself before, through its physical senses, up to the final lucid moments in this earthly life.

The continuing existence of both this self-determined will, and of the consciousness revealed within that will, unquestionably suffices to call the subsequent condition a *survival* of that being's life; for physical existence, too, is but the tangibly perceived expression of a timeless will, determined by its individuated form, and thus defined alike by its own consciousness.

But no thinking mind could rightly be expected to believe that man's surviving will— or the given consciousness attained within this self-formed will—shall find itself at once transported to spheres of everlasting bliss when mortal life has ended, or could be simply hurled among the damned to suffer endless torments.

Nor shall the timeless individuality, which used to manifest itself within a mortal body, now suddenly escape to some abode above the clouds or to the stars.

What does occur is nothing other than a change in man's perceptive faculties. As a result, the consciousness of the eternal will, which now is free from the restraints of physical perception, henceforth can employ the senses of its spiritual organism. Even during mortal life it is this very organism to which man is indebted for all his spiritual life and knowledge, whether it be rich or insignificant.

But as for that which man initially encounters after he has lost his mortal organism and its senses, it is described already in detail in the preceding chapter of this book.

DESPITE ALL THE VARIETIES that it embraces, the manner of perception is identical in all domains of spiritual existence, from the very lowest sphere up to the sublimest, inmost world of light.

The difference lies merely in the forms that are perceived, and in the clarity that individuals possess in apprehending what they see within a given realm.

The more advanced a person's self-awareness, the more distinctly shall his individuated will—whose form is now that of a radiant crystal—perceive itself, within its proper consciousness, as the *creator* of its own eternal world within the light and substance of the

Spirit. The more directly, too, shall then the absolute Reality, the source of all that ultimately *is,* reveal its very nature to that person's inmost consciousness.

Only a chaotic will, one still devoid of form and structure and, therefore, in the dark about itself, would ever tend toward *formless* being.

A self-possessed and clearly structured will, however, which in itself embodies order in rhythm and proportion can only manifest itself again in forms of harmony and order wherever it seeks self-expression. Indeed, self-structured will finds its sublimest joy in realizing, in everything it is creating, the highest level of perfection that is potentially contained in its creation.

Every real artist, but also many others who are creative in their work, can sense a faint reflection of such joy. But only in the Spirit's world is granted true fulfillment to that which here on earth the human soul perceives as through a veil.

To discipline his *will*—by using its own formative potential—is, for this reason, the human being's first and most important inner task. It is the first step on the way that in the end will lead him to the inmost realm within the Spirit.

TRULY, WE ARE CLOSER to you than you know. Indeed, we are with you wherever you may be; for that in you which is already *of the Spirit is* present even now inside the Spirit's world we see and know. Only you are not yet able to sense your own identity with that which you are *in the Spirit*.

Before you can experience this identity, your timeless will must first have reached perfection. It must have found its purest form, and manifest itself in conscious harmony and order.

Only those who tirelessly labor to escape the darkened labyrinths in which confused ideas about the Spirit's life, its nature and reality, still hold them blindly captive, only they shall one day know the clarity of spiritual light, in which we live and breathe.

Having found this light, the seeking soul will also comprehend why all the questions that, at the beginning of the way, it used to ask in vain can find a wholly satisfying answer only at the journey's end.

This also is the reason why all guidance to the Spirit's life must first require that the soul have *faith*. For faith is the dynamic energy wherein orginates the impulse to *advance*.

At the beginning of the way that leads him to the *Temple of Eternity* the pupil must have faith. For knowledge comes to those alone who have attained the journey's goal.

One who has no faith that he is *able* one day to attain his highest goal will hardly be prepared to bear the burden that he will have to carry on this way. And he that will not take this burden on himself shall surely not be granted certitude in matters of the Spirit during life on earth.

Such certitude, however, you have the power to attain; even though you cannot enter yet the Spirit's inmost realm while you still live this present life.

But having gained objective knowledge in the Spirit, one has accomplished infinitely more than if he had acquired all the wisdom of this world.

In what *we* are he shall perceive his *own* eternal self and, *one* with *us*, the realms of light shall now be also *his* eternal home.

It would be very wrong to think, however, that spiritual knowledge is gained by only those who haughtily dismiss all worldly learning and scoff at the achievements of man's intellect.

While it is true that spiritual knowledge is not attained through mental effort, it nonetheless can guide the mind toward many new discoveries.

Spiritual insights may not be found the way that one discovers scientific facts. But mental knowledge, too, can never be acquired except by effort of the mind.

What human intellect can learn by way of physical investigation can never be an object of spiritual experience. Nor could there ever be a contradiction between these different approaches toward obtaining knowledge, except such contradictions were due to faulty thinking.

Yet knowledge based on spiritual perception is only found where all things that the mind creates have vanished—beyond the province of the intellect.

CHAPTER THREE

THE ONLY
ABSOLUTE
REALITY

I HOPE THAT YOU MAY now already have begun to sense, however faintly, a trace of the mysterious realm of absolute Reality, in which all final causes are eternally begot and born, and which reveals itself—in infinite abundance of phenomena—in all domains that are experienced through perception, no matter by which senses they might be perceived.

But perhaps your inner senses are still not keen enough, because you never thought to sharpen their perception?

Then you probably still sense but little of the mystery this book seeks to disclose to you. Or else you do not read my words as I would have you read them?

It is my wish, however, that you learn to *see,* so that you will not one day have to enter the domain of Spirit like one who still is blinded by illusions when the time has come that you must leave this present life.

Avidyâ—ignorance—is rightly judged by Eastern wisdom as a wrong that burdens man with moral guilt; for nothing but your own free *will* can ever shut the gate through which you could reach timeless knowledge.

As you have heard now more than once in the foregoing, your present world of *physical* perception is divided from the world of Spirit only by a barrier that separates two kinds of fundamentally dissimilar *perceptions.* I have intentionally repeated this already several times, and I likewise shall have to repeat it in what follows, in order that this basic fact become as firmly rooted in your mind as possible.

Thus, I here again have to remind you that absolute Reality itself remains forever *One* —the final cause of all that is—even though it is perceived by the most varied faculties, both in the world of *physical* and that of *spiritual* phenomena.

Philosophical speculation has intuitively sensed the fact of this Reality, and called it *the-thing-in-itself*.

But speculative thought, however deep and penetrating, can never even vaguely fathom ultimate Reality as such.

Practical experience alone can comprehend it; but no one can attain this practical experience except the few who proved themselves authentic *masters* of this ancient and most secret way of knowing.

And these alone can also guide their own successors to attain this practical experience; but those they choose to follow them have, like themselves, been born with the capacity for knowing such experience.

The present writer, too, has found what can be known about these matters in that way.

Who, then, but one of us could ever in your present life bring you authentic witness—at least to the extent that words permit—of that which is the only absolute Reality: the final cause of all phenomena?

Let me try and see, then, whether I can reach your understanding. I never shall succeed, however, unless your inner sense and feeling seek to grasp what I convey; for only if that inmost part of you that in itself is *of the Spirit* shall sense its own self in my words can you find lasting truth and certainty.

Today your vision is still blinded by the brilliance of a passing light that truly has the power to blind mortal eyes.

Before all else you first must learn to *see*.

Your eyes must gain their freedom: they must be free to show you what you *want* to see, instead of being forced to see no more than that which to most people is the *only* thing they see.

Your eyes must learn to see *within* as clearly as they now can only see *without*.

However, it is not alone a different kind of "seeing"; rather, your entire inner life, your faculty for *feeling* things will have to undergo a gradual renewal.

The way in which you sense your own *existence* must be liberated from the fetters that still shackle you today—if you would clearly and unfailingly discern, within yourself, the absolute Reality: the final cause of all *phenomena* that manifest themselves throughout Creation.

THREADS OF MAGIC ENERGY pervade the fabric of even this external world of physical perception, and if you are persistent in your efforts of learning how to "see" *within,* you will in time be able to distinguish the *phenomena* of physical existence from what are the creative *elements* of absolute Reality, which manifest themselves in this external world.

You then will be astonished to discover that ultimate Reality, which is the final cause of all things that exist, can be *experienced* also in this world of physical phenomena; namely, in the form of what are in effect the hidden, spiritual *elements* of Being. While many people have experienced the workings of these elements, many others still deny that they exist because they never sensed them in their proper consciousness.

None who has been granted the experience of which I speak could ever be disturbed again by others' doubts and skepticism. Moreover, his experience will guard him from confusing these purely *spiritual* elements with forces stemming from the unseen sphere of *physical* perception, even though both kinds of energies are commonly referred to as "occult," as "mystical," or "supernatural."

All of the physical universe around you, including your own body, is constructed from the visible *effects* of spiritual elements that, hidden from your mortal senses, emanate from the domain of Being, the realm of absolute Reality. And in the same way, all the worlds in the domain of Spirit are but the manifest, perceived effects of these same elements of timeless Being.

It merely is the difference in our manner of perception that makes us apprehend the manifest effects of these creative elements either as the world of *matter* or as the realm of *spirit*.

You now will understand that the "beyond" is not an altogether different world, originating in a separate cause, but only the result of

what to you is still a new and unfamiliar manner of *perceiving*: of apprehending the effects
of these mysterious elements, whose tangible
results in physical existence you have become
accustomed to see as "life on earth."

Your consciousness does not "create" Reality,
because your consciousness itself is but a part
of this Reality; that is to say, it is itself but one
of the creative, spiritual *elements* of Being.
However, both in this existence and in the
worlds beyond, your consciousness is the
creator of *phenomena* and of your manner of
perceiving them. Yet the phenomena as such,
which you are able to perceive, are brought
about—in either realm—as the effects of
these creative *elements* of Being.

In order for you to experience *physical* reality,
these elemental forces must manifest themselves in one specific way. You are already
quite familiar with this way, in that it is the
function of your body's senses.

By virtue of the senses that you here possess,
all of your experience—your grasp of temporal reality—is precisely given and determined; and so you only can perceive what

things your faculties *allow* you to perceive—and nothing more.

But since you are yourself a part of absolute Reality—as a drop of water in the sea is a component of the sea—you, too, potentially contain within you all the properties of absolute Reality: as every drop of the sea contains the essence of that sea.

Therefore, you are able to perceive not only through the senses of your mortal body; for as you are yourself of spiritual origin, yours also is a spiritual organism, here and in eternity.

In your spiritual body you are given faculties that are unknown to you at present; these inner faculties, however, are close equivalents of what in earthly life you call your *senses*.

Once you live "beyond," you will create your own domain—your world of spiritual perception—by virtue of your spiritual senses; exactly as, in physical existence, *you* create the form in which this temporal reality is apprehended by your present senses. To be sure, you are not now aware that this is so.

To assist your understanding, consider for a moment a person in hypnotic trance.

In this state he sees, hears, and feels whatever you will make him apprehend: through your power of suggestion. Yet, to himself all of his experiences are completely *real*.

You are convinced that he deceives himself by an illusion you imposed on him; however, it is you who are deceived in this assumption.

All you have done was to release the person for a certain time from the compulsion of taking only that for "real" which he perceives by virtue of his mortal senses; and thus he now can for brief moments also see, hear, and feel through his spiritual faculties, if you so instruct him. And in this way he brings into existence whatever you direct him to perceive.

It is not you that shows him what he sees; nor, to be sure, can he see anything of that which in the world of spiritual perception is collectively experienced by all those who inhabit this domain.

You merely guide the powers of his *plastic*, his *formative*, imagination; and since he now

—his physical perception being blocked—can also use his spiritual senses, *his* will endows with shape and being—out of spiritual substance and for a little while—what are *equivalents* of all the images that you have caused his will to reproduce.

It is not the wooden staff with which you touch his hand—while you suggest it is a red-hot iron—that has raised the blister on his hand. Instead, the blister is produced by his experience of the spiritually perceived equivalent of an objective rod of red-hot iron. Now this rod could cause the blister only for the reason that its spiritual equivalent, which did produce it, is ultimately based upon the same mysterious elements that constitute what is the absolute Reality behind all manifest phenomena.

The person who is hypnotized will never for an instant doubt that the experience, which he himself created, was absolutely *real*. And if you told him to remember what he saw and felt also after he awakened, he will at that time not be able to believe that what he did experience had not occurred within the world of physical perception.

However, his experiences could only be so very real because they ultimately rested on the same Reality as those of physical perception, with which he *is* familiar.

ALTHOUGH HYPNOSIS HAS been used here only for the sake of illustration, and while the insights it provides into the realm of spiritual perception are rather limited and superficial, it nonetheless may serve as an example to show you that your present form of sense perception, that is, through your body's faculties, is not the only way in which you can be conscious.

Here on earth, as mortal humans, all of us live in a state of, as it were, *collective hypnosis*. As a result, we are not able to perceive except what our "hypnotizer"—our own incarnate will—allows us to perceive. Yet our will would not be found within the physical dimension, unless its driving impulse were expressly seeking self-experience in the realm of physical expression.

As soon as we have learned to turn our innate will around—which now is still directed toward the realm of time and matter—we shall become acquainted with the laws of other kinds of sense perception.

While only few are able to accomplish this reversal in the course of mortal life, all must of necessity confront it when death deprives their will of its material organs of perception.

All man's fear of death results from the un-willingness of his eternal will—now directed toward the realm of matter—to turn itself around: reversing the direction it had taken after what became its "fall" from the domain of timeless light.

You now will understand why one who in this life has *not* awakened yet in the domain of Spirit initially can only grope his way into a *border realm* in life beyond: a realm that cor-responds to concepts and ideas which he and others of like mind had fashioned. Before he can be guided upward, to reach the Spirit's highest world—the world of absolute fulfill-ment—he first must have become both mas-ter of himself and of his timeless will.

Nor have we room for anyone who has not given up all selfish aims and wishes. Because his very presence in the realm of Spirit we possess and share would mean its plunging into night and chaos—were it possible that any such could ever rise to the sublimest world in the eternal.

Perhaps you now will see why earlier I pointed out that all of us are here united into one collective will, a will that never can be changed in its direction.

By UNIFYING OUR INDIVIDUAL will with that of absolute Reality, wherein each single will is conscious of its own existence only as embodying the will of all, we have become unchallenged sovereigns of absolute Reality within the worlds of spirit.

Thus we knowingly became creators of what is the sublimest realm within the worlds of spiritual perception.

Insofar as one can speak of the perfectibility of a condition that has neither a beginning nor an end, in that it always is both things at once, we know that our own perfection rests on the continuous, self-conscious *forming* and *sustaining* of that which is the highest and most radiant world of spiritual perception: the very plane on which we build and work, and where we also find the *Temple* for our worship.

What we *are* is only that which our unified, eternal will is willing us to *be*.

THE "WILL" ONE SPEAKS OF in the ordinary language of this life is no more than a wish or a desire, or the expression of some inclination inspired by a function of the mind.

If mortal man's eternal will were subject to his wishes, then every wish and each desire would of necessity be answered and fulfilled.

But this is not what happens, as everyone well knows. Indeed, we can thank heaven on our knees that in this life not every wish has power to command a will.

In earthly life our timeless will is willing only to express itself within specific *limitations*, which are imposed on it because it *sought* existence in the world of matter. To be sure, the wishes of the mortal mind would be only too happy to rescind these limitations whenever it should suit them.

Only in the Spirit's world, the realm perceived through other senses, is our will at liberty to alter its direction.

There the spell of physical "hypnosis" has been broken and other senses of perception with which man is endowed are able to reveal themselves.

Here again you will discover why it is absurd to think that people who departed from this life could ever "rematerialize" in order to communicate with those who are still living.

For this would mean that one who has at last been liberated from the shackles of his physical perception could once again fall victim to this limitation.

Even if it were not violating any laws of nature, the person could no longer *will* such a "return," because his conscious will has long since freed itself from its hypnotic spell. Besides, he would require a living physical organism before he could in fact experience physical existence.

As I explained before, all the apparitions conjured up in spiritualist séances, which many people take for the "materialized" entelechy of a departed mortal—or, for that matter, any other kind of physical manifestation occurring in such sittings—are nothing more than the activity of beings that, as a rule, are hidden from man's physical perception, but nonetheless belong entirely to the domain of *physical* reality.

Although their organism is invisible, it is not in any way of spiritual substance; nor are these beings even conscious of the realm of Spirit.

However, in their given physical organism, which mortal man can normally not see, they have senses of quite extraordinary sharpness; senses that are physical in nature, and thus can only bring forth physical perception, but even so surpass by far the keenness of all faculties possessed by man.

In addition, these creatures are endowed with faculties that mortal man does not possess, a lack for which he seeks to compensate, as best he may, by using sundry technical devices.

ALTHOUGH THE BEINGS that I speak of are invisible to human eyes, certain animals can apprehend their presence very clearly. These creatures, then, are able—for brief periods, and by their using human energies—to realize *material* forms, which then are of necessity perceived by mortal eyes as well.

They can produce, and then employ, such forms by merging their own will with that of certain human beings, the so-called *mediums,* while at the same time draining off the latter's "psyche," that is to say, their *temporal* or *animal* "soul."

In some respects these occult creatures, which live beyond the range of physical perception, are rather similar to man; however, at no time have they in fact been human beings, nor will they ever be.

Their position relative to *man's* invisible material body is, rather, that which animals in nature occupy in contrast to man's outer organism.

The proper sphere of action nature has allotted to these beings lies in the inner realms of physical creation, and here they weave and build behind the world of matter.

The "goblins" and "gnomes" or the sprites of water, earth, and sea that people fairy tales and legends are frequently depicted in a manner which makes it very reasonable to suspect that—allowing for the obvious additions due to popular imagination—these tales are not so much invented fables as records of experience.

To call these forces "spirits" must not, of course, obscure the fact that one is dealing here with beings which are wholly physical. To them the realm of Spirit is not merely barred; indeed, they are not even conscious that it does exist.

Only ignorance about the facts behind these matters may excuse one who can seriously consider, if not indeed believe, that he communicates with *human* spirits in spiritualist séances.

To be sure, beings of the Spirit's world, including the departed, *can* under certain circumstances make themselves both seen and heard; however, you will then perceive them only with your *spiritual* senses, even though you think you see and hear them with your eyes and ears.

But never under any circumstances shall a being from the Spirit's world cause anything to move or happen in the realm of physics.

In order that you may perceive a spiritual being—through your inner senses—it is necessary that one free you, temporarily, from the hypnotic spell of physical perception; and this will be effected from the spiritual side.

Those who are about you, but are not similarly influenced, will then see neither the figure that you see, nor hear the words you hear; and yet, what you have seen and heard need not by any means be mere "hallucination"; for this would, after all, be only the effect of your imagination: a phantom of your plastic fantasy.

If you are granted an authentic spiritual experience—without your having sought it—you should accept it with due reverence and guard within your heart what you were privileged to witness.

However, it would be unwise to desire any such experience; for one must have attained a high degree of critical discernment to be able clearly to distinguish genuine perceptions of your spiritual senses from what are merely vividly perceived hallucinations. And, surely, your intent is not to see a "ghost" that very well might simply be an image of yourself, projected to perform behind a hollow mask.

The cases of authentic apprehension through spiritual senses are so extremely rare that one is well advised *not* to believe that one has had a true experience from spiritual regions unless severest critical examination can definitely exclude the likelihood that one's experience was purely a hallucination.

However, absolutely certain judgment in these matters can only be acquired through long and wide experience; it follows that one cannot have such judgment unless one's spiritual senses are already permanently opened.

What has been called "clairvoyance" is *not* the faculty of seeing anything of spiritual reality.

All the clairvoyant "seer" sees are things belonging to the physical world, although they may be far away in time or space. Sometimes this includes the world's invisible domain, together with the occult beings that inhabit it, and which he then considers to be "spirits."

A clairvoyant may provide the most astounding proofs of his capacity for seeing distant things, even the past and the future: he never will see anything except events connected with the world of *physical* perception.

The visions he describes, which he believes are *spiritual* realities, are either the unseen dimensions of this physical domain, or mere delusions, generated by his own capacity for shaping plastic images. In either case he feels convinced that what he sees must be objective witness of the Spirit's world.

In the latter case his visions will invariably be colored by the views and prejudices that occupy his mind in daily life.

If he is a Christian, he will tell you that he saw the sacred persons of the Gospel, or saints the Church has canonized; if he grew up with concepts of Indian religious systems he will believe he saw the gods of Brahmanism, and in Tibet those of the Mahâyâna school.

Numberless mirages and delusions presenting life "beyond" already have been spread by so-called seers among the many who are eager to believe, and to this day such fictions are accepted as pure fact by minds who in their innocence infer that a clairvoyant who has shown that he can see into the past or future must, for this reason, surely know the realm of Spirit.

The organ that permits clairvoyant sight is no more than a rudimentary *physical* organ, a vestige that survived from mankind's earliest beginnings on this planet.

As instances of "atavism" this organ can at times recur, and function tolerably well, also in people of the present age.

All "clairvoyance," "clairaudience," and "clairsentience" is merely the result of being able to employ this unknown physical organ.

Here should also be included what has been called "psychometrie"—the gift of seeing the history of an object after merely touching it—

as well as many a variety of "fortune telling," even though the mode that is employed here may, purposely or unintentionally, conceal the "seer's" real practices.

THAT YOU MAY LEARN TO comprehend what life "beyond" is in reality, you must begin by recognizing *three* domains within the cosmos.

First, there is the realm of *physical* perception, or the world of matter.

Then there is the realm of *spiritual* perception, or the world of the Spirit.

Third, however, there is the domain of the mysterious, cause-effecting elements of Being: the only absolute Reality, as whose effect exist all forms of sense perception, and their respective worlds, both in the physical as in the spiritual dimensions of the cosmos.

These hidden, cause-effecting elements of Being are manifest in mortal man as the component "forces" of his timeless soul.

Once having crystallized around a human will, and thus collectively assuming form for the duration of a human life, these forces take on, as it were, the individual's specific temperament and coloring, as it is manifested in his timeless will. And thus their character becomes determined for all time, so that they henceforth must obey the given impulse until it has attained fulfillment.

If this fulfillment is denied them in the lifetime of the person who imbued them with their now exclusive impulse, these forces of man's timeless soul will manifest themselves again and again: seeking to achieve their end in other human lives, until they finally attain fulfillment by being *unified* with the eternal will of an incarnate mortal, and thus becoming *one* with him.

Owing to a wrong interpretation of what they had observed concerning these realities, Eastern people were misled into believing that man's immortal *self* is many times reborn and reembodied on this earth.

But such reembodiment 7—that is to say, a *falling back* into the self-hypnosis of physical perception—is possible only in three cases: one, where man has consciously and with premeditation destroyed his mortal body: a deed which never is an act of man's eternal will, but merely an attempt at "breaking out" inspired by frustrated wishes; second, where a child has died before his timeless will has had a chance to reach fulfillment of its drive toward knowing life in physical perception; and, third, where someone's drive toward physical experience was so abnormally intense that even the death of his physical body could only interrupt this self-hypnosis for a little while.

Thus, the doctrine of "reincarnation" does not apply to normal circumstances any more than death in infancy, or suicide, may be regarded as the normally appointed end of human life on earth.

If you experience memories, or even faint impressions, that would persuade you to assume that you have lived on earth before, you may perhaps be right in this belief and thus in fact exemplify one of the exceptions under which a reembodiment may actually occur. Yet in your present life you would do better to leave this question open; for only in your spiritual existence will you be able to receive the answer.

The impression that you once lived on this earth as someone *other* than yourself is most assuredly always a deception; for in the mentioned special cases, which alone admit of a repeated incarnation on this earth, it always is the selfsame individuality that is embodied, and thus is seeking its own self-experience in the realm of physical perception.

On the other hand, one may consider it as nearly certain that every individual whose inner sensibilities are not completely numbed will at times have felt that there were forces seeking to assert themselves within his soul that had received their impulses by human beings who had lived in earlier times, and which were still pursuing their fulfillment.

Where this is taking place the individual may well experience memories of striking visual reality; however, these originated in the lives of those who in their time had given the specific impulse to these forces, which then were in *their* soul, but now continue to be active in another human life.

It is not difficult to understand why someone who has had such an experience would then become convinced that he himself had been the author of such memories, which still preserve what he believes had once occurred in *his* existence. Nonetheless, such a belief is based on only superficial observation and rests on very shaky ground.

EVERY SINGLE HUMAN BEING is a unique, original, and individuated emanation of eternal Will. It has proceeded from the timeless "Sea of Godhead yet unformed" in order that it realize its individual perfection, whose form is different from that of every other of its fellow emanations.

Any person who is born on earth and thus must bear the labors, pains, and tribulations inseparably bound up with existence in an animal organism, has brought this fate upon himself. For by his own free will he interrupted the ascent to his perfection in the world of light: because he sought this self-experience in the domain of physical perception.

But sooner or later necessity will force him to turn back, and then he shall resume his rise toward the perfection of his spiritual form.

The earlier he recognizes, already in his life on earth, what is the only way to end his anguished searches, the more support and benefit he will be able to derive from life on earth: for all his future progress toward perfection; and the easier it will be to remove, already in his present life, the many obstacles that else may later on severely hinder his advance on that ascent.

Yet even though a mortal human cannot, in this present life, awaken to the conscious use of his eternal spiritual faculties, a great deal is achieved already if he has been instructed and informed—by those among his fellow mortals who can employ their spiritual faculties—about the real structure of man's life "beyond": the form of being that awaits him after the conclusion of his life on earth.

Throughout the realm that is experienced by means of physical senses it is the same kind of perception whereby phenomena are caused and apprehended. And yet, there are vast differences between the world seen by a bird or ant and that perceived by you. In the same way, there are enormous differences between the realms perceived by the entelechies who can employ their *spiritual* faculties.

Just as there are many worlds of physical perception, so there are countless worlds in the domain of Spirit.

The individuated, timeless will of man, however, shall find the absolute perfection of its being only when it has been able to unite itself—down to the last remaining atom of its self—with that which is the Will behind the All: *one* within the innermost domain of Spirit, the realm of cause-effecting elements of Being; *one* within the kingdom of aeonic Light: the only absolute Reality.

Beyond this world of worlds there is left nothing more the human being can experience; for this sublimest of all realms of light is infinite in time and space, and also in the wealth of the fulfillments that it offers.

To the extent that *unformed* Being—the boundless and unfathomable Sea of Godhead—is accessible at all to the perception of a conscious *will* endowed with *form*—which thus is finite as to space, though infinite in time—it can only be in this sublimest world of light that unformed Being will reveal its very self: within the consciousness of each and every individuated Will, which in this realm is one with all.

What I attempted to explain in the preceding chapters embraces everything that man on earth can comprehend of the profoundest mystery of his existence, both here and in the world awaiting him beyond.

All things else you may have heard about that other life—whether they be phantoms born in fervid ecstasies of faith, or products of mere speculation—are nothing more than baseless theories and idle fiction.

But you should not "believe" in theories and speculative world views just because some other people take such notions for the truth; for never shall *your* soul experience lasting peace until you found yourself again: as the eternal self-expression of what is absolute Reality.

CHAPTER FOUR

WHAT
SHOULD
ONE DO?

I N THE TRILOGY comprising *The Book on the Living God, The Book on Life Beyond,* and *The Book on Human Nature* I have for the first time shown in great detail, each step along the inner way that those must take who earnestly would find their spiritual life and nature in themselves.

In these three books I clearly outlined what those who take this path must do, and what they must avoid.

All this notwithstanding, there are readers who keep asking me: "What, exactly, should we do? How are we to begin?"

From the way their questions are expressed and motivated it becomes apparent that what such readers wish to have are: itemized instructions for the performance of some "exercise"—the more mysterious the better—which is guaranteed to bring them tangible results if they will just repeat it every day, more or less mechanically.

But when answering such questions my dilemma is the same as that of many a physician who only recommends the simplest and most natural remedies, and thereby leaves some patients disappointed because he did not write them a "prescription."

The majority of those who have such questions on their minds, nor ever cease to ask them, had earlier set out on ways that were to lead them into the bewildering labyrinth of modern theosophical and occult literature. Only thanks to their good sense and healthy instincts had they finally escaped that maze again, but not without a struggle and great effort.

But while such readers may earlier have been misled, their search was not without some gain. For there is no mistake that might not in the end, if by a somewhat longer route, still guide an earnest seeker to the truth.

For this reason, none should curse the time he was in error, because he does not know how much he owes to past mistakes.

So, too, such groping through the crypts of theosophical, anthroposophical, or occult theories and dogmas has not been wholly wasted for those who in the end regained their inner freedom.

For, owing to their former searches, many came to be convinced that underneath all the erroneous beliefs they had encountered on those paths there had to be some core of hidden truth.

In others there began to dawn the insight that the very legend of the so-called Mahâtmas— the mysterious, supposed founders of present-day Theosophy—could only have arisen because the Orient knows of the existence of certain individuals who truly are united with and in the Spirit. Beings who do not perform the sort of fakir tricks ascribed to the fictitious masters of Theosophy, but are, indeed, completely conscious in the spirit, already in their mortal life.

On the other hand, most people who had groped their way around the murky crypts of occultism had brought from there as well the curious belief that all one needed was to be instructed in a secret and, doubtless, thoroughly mysterious "technique," which, if known, would raise a common human mortal forthwith to the level of a "seer" of higher worlds, make him an "initiate," if not, indeed, a real *Master*, one of those that have the power to effect events in the domain of Spirit.

CORRECT AS THE TWO former suppositions are, the latter is, of course, absurd.

Nonetheless, unconscionable charlatans and clever hunters after human souls have profited from this particular belief, and thus have given to their pupils a variety of more or less suspicious precepts, which they themselves had picked from ancient tracts on mysticism. As a rule, the teacher of such secret lore is himself completely in the dark concerning the effects that such instructions may produce if they are faithfully obeyed.

The pupil, on the other hand, feels certain that the path on which he finds himself is right; for, after all, he sees that one can really obtain results if one will follow the instructions he was given. Results, indeed, still puzzling to the professional psychologist, despite all recent explorations of the human psyche and all the probing into man's subconscious.

More than one among the propagators of such occult "science" may only satisfy his vanity when he is passing on instructions to "open inner senses," which he unearthed from some forgotten tome. Practices which will unlock no more in man than vaults of occult putrefaction, where nothing thrives except an active form of mediumship: an eerie craft that one had better leave to certain Asian sorcerers.

The oracular purveyor of such occult practices need not himself believe in the effectiveness of his instructions.

Just as carriers of germs may be in perfect health, and still spread the most devastating plague, so, too, the teacher of such methods for the alleged "unfolding" of man's inner senses need never know that all he does to his poor victims is to make them active *mediums*.

For the disciples of such banes of divers stripe it is, however, very easy to deal with any scientific criticism; for they can see from every comment of their learned critics how innocently such most honorable minds experiment in a domain where one mirage succeeds another, and where the self-assured experimenter is at every turn lured deeper into the morass, while growing ever more convinced that he is but one step away from solving the great mystery.

ONE MIGHT HAVE ONLY welcomed the latest efforts undertaken by professional psychologists in order to devalue certain highly questionable "supernatural" phenomena. Regrettably, these efforts were themselves devalued by the false conclusions the scientists had drawn from otherwise undoubtedly correct and valid observations. Their mistakes are plainly obvious, however, to anyone who is sufficiently acquainted with the subject.

Even though a person's thirst for knowledge and for truth be of impeccable integrity, if prejudices hold him captive, his search for light will lead him into error.

The outcome is that the disciples who surround the sundry hunters of bewildered souls, which stumble in the dark of cloudy notions, have long since given up all hope of finding truth in the pursuit of scientific disciplines. Instead, they eagerly allow themselves to be impressed—and duped—by every traveling occult jester who shrewdly hawks his merchandise as a secret, esoteric "science."

And if the methods taught by such a teacher actually produce the growth of mediumistic sensibilities of which I spoke, his triumph is complete. For now his faithful would not dream of doubting whatever veiled suggestions he might drop, intimating that he was the now "returned" and "reincarnate" spirit of some sublime immortal from the past.

Anyone who read my warnings with some judgment will long have recognized not only that I am acquainted with all the mentioned old and recent secret "methods," but that I also could quite easily provide, beyond those touched upon, some other ways to further the unfolding of such "higher" senses; ways that none of the peculiar mystagogues had ever heard about who nowadays are seen by their disciples as "initiates" and "scientific experts" in the field of occult lore.

There are methods that produce results which even the most gifted pupils of the like initiates would think beyond their powers. Results that also would be sure to baffle even an ingenious specialist of psychological analysis.

Were it not a crime beyond atonement to even hint at the respective, very dangerous paths, a word or two might well suffice to clear up more than one phenomenon that neither psychological experiments nor metaphysical research have yet been able to explain.

But though I wish I could perform this service for psychology, I am, alas, not free to do so. Not merely for the reason that disclosure would be criminal, nor owing to the obligations by which I and my spiritual equals are bound on earth and in eternity, but also since this is a field that calls for much more than mere scientific zeal if one would enter it with true authority.

It hardly will be necessary to point out that what I have in mind are not the practices of *Hatha Yoga*, which have long been common knowledge, nor any method based on them, which likewise can be turned to working certain fakir tricks.

BUT EVEN IF I WERE NOT bound in any way, I still could never bring myself to lift the veil from what is hidden for compelling reasons. For well I know what evils would inevitably follow if ever knowledge of this kind should fall into the hands of individuals who hunger after power.

But, then, I am not anxious to incur the "torments of Prometheus," which would inexorably be my fate if I became the author of such horrors.

In order to attain the spiritual union with *Eternal Light*—to raise man's timeless nature from its earthly sleep—for that event which light-inspired knowledge means by man's *rebirth* all such things are neither needed nor of the slightest use.

Like all the other skills that rest upon the application of a certain, ordinarily unknown, psycho-physical potential of energies kept in a state of heightened tension, those practices of which I speak have likewise nothing whatsoever to do with the awakening of what is man's *eternal* self.

What is required for the sake of this awakening is, first and foremost, the attainment of a constant orientation of all one's thinking, one's emotions, and one's temporal desires, all of which must be directed towards the mentioned goal.

The human being as a whole must first have gradually transformed *itself,* and through its proper energies, before it can be reached by truly *spiritual* help.

It is of little use, or none at all, to realize this orientation only from time to time, such as many faithful are accustomed to devoting one day out of seven to the worship of their God.

Every minute of one's further life, every single action done throughout the day, every thought that comes to mind, and every wish

and impulse of one's mortal—mentally determined—will must henceforth be subordi-
nated to the guiding influence of the
demanded orientation: if one who means to
take this path is to experience *real* progress,
not merely dreams of his imagination.

Periodic exercises can at best renew one's
concentration on that goal and thereby
strengthen the resolve to seek the needed
orientation.

Whatever may be recommended to this end is
only for one purpose: to help maintain, within
the center of one's consciousness, the state of
inner orientation of all one's thoughts and
feelings, so that it will not be forgotten for one
moment.

If this inner state is constantly maintained,
however, so that its influence is manifested
every second of one's daily life, no matter by
what means—which may be suited to one's
temperament—this goal has been achieved,
then all the rest will follow of *itself,* that is to
say, without our conscious effort.

For, in a person of such inner firmness there comes to life a *nucleus* of spiritual energy and this will grow in strength until it finally comes into conscious contact with similar, but perfectly developed nuclei of that same spiritual energy, which manifests itself on earth through certain individuals. Such contact is established without a special effort of the person's will.

Once that contact is established, the awakening soul receives the help of those who have already reached man's final goal, and who now see no higher duty than helping those who are already able to receive their help, even if the latter are not yet aware of this within their mental consciousness.

The awakening soul has now become what, for the sake of illustration, may be compared to a *receiver* for a specific kind of spiritual *transmission*. To be sure, the energies that are transmitted here can only be perceived by *spiritual* senses. No physical experiment can, therefore, ever prove that they exist.

Events originating in the realm of spiritual substance are only known through individual experience: by man's becoming *one* with them. They never can be treated as material for experiments that are designed to help detached observers formulate some learned definitions. Spiritual events are *living energies*; they instantly withdraw if one makes but the slightest move to interfere with them.

You should not think, however, that one can easily become such a receiver, or that one does it overnight.

To be accepted as a true apprentice by those whose craft is timeless, a soul must be prepared to garb herself in patience.

Even the most energetic, physically engendered "will" cannot accelerate the growth of our faculties for spiritual perception, because this kind of will is only the result of mental functions. And these must never be confused with man's *eternal* will, which is of spiritual substance and manifests itself in his immortal essence.

Indeed, a stubborn, hardened, mentally engendered will should only hinder the crystallizing process of the energies involved. For these are now to rearrange themselves spontaneously into a differently structured entity, that is to say, an organism that will not be subject to the strictures of the mortal brain.

By contrast, the more firmly one will realize the mentioned orientation of one's entire self—in the way a telescope remains directed towards its object—the sooner one shall reach the point at which the soul can consciously perceive the inner contact with those who help her from the realm of Spirit.

In other words, the only thing that matters here is man's effective conduct in his ordinary daily life—not the performance or nonperformance of especial exercises.

That does not mean, however, that it would be wrong to follow any form of meditative practice, at periodic intervals, if one has found that this will help more firmly to maintain the needed state of mind, and consciously to hold it focused on the inner goal.

Once having gained sufficient contact with the spiritual helpers, the person's inner energies are first examined in a kind of test. Its outcome will determine the form of spiritual influence best suited to his future guidance.

Such inner guidance can take many forms, extending from the simple reinforcement of a person's own capacities, to the highest rank of individuated teaching.

The very few who had already known this guidance long before their present mortal life—because on earth they are to work as *masters* in the Spirit's timeless craft—attain at last a state of absolute identity with their respective teacher, even though he may be living on a different continent. And at this point the pupil is no longer taught through words and concepts, but partakes directly of his teacher's spiritual—not of his mental—consciousness.

If the teacher would that some events, occurring in *his* spirit, be consciously experienced also by his pupil, his mere intention is sufficient for the latter to perceive them just as though they were occurring in *himself*. To be sure, the pupil always clearly knows to whom he is indebted for the like experience.

Given that his master—for his own entelechy—has long since realized the union
with *Eternal Light,* the pupil's first experience of that union occurs in being one in
spirit with his teacher's radiantly enlightened
soul.

Gradually the pupil, too, becomes mature
enough to realize this union with *Eternal
Light* himself, so that he can attain it on his
own.

Having reached this goal, he is no longer only
conscious of his own eternally imperishable
being, but at the same time takes part in the
conscious life of every individuated spiritual
self that ever came to manifest itself in human
form, like him.

Once perfected in this way, the pupil's self-
awareness is now participating in a—to him
still new—collective consciousness, which
embraces every individuated self that has
attained this goal before him. Yet to describe
this state of consciousness there are no physical analogies.

The pupil's knowledge of himself from now on
rests embedded in a form of self-awareness

that unifies the individuated consciousness of all.

But never could the individuated self of one who has attained perfection become dissolved in that collective self-awareness.

Instead, embodied in this union, the individuated self lives henceforth, here and in eternity, the life of one and all: infusing all the other individualities and, equally, infused by them. And yet, united in this way no spiritual self could ever lose its own distinct identity, which is determined by its proper will.

CONSIDERING THE GIVEN structure of Reality, one cannot help that final certainty respecting the survival of man's consciousness after the loss of his physical body, and thus his self-experience in the realm of spiritual perception, can only be attained by those few mortals who have achieved the mentioned goal already, in this present life.

Everyone else can only theorize about that life, indulge in pure assumptions, or look for comfort in the promises of some religious creed. Unless, that is, he cares to trust the witness of those few among his fellow men who know that future life already, from permanent experience.

Unprejudiced, discerning judgment will readily distinguish between authentic revelations—offered by the few that had attained this goal in actual fact, not merely in a state of mental rapture, nor spell-bound by some method of hypnosis—and the many fanciful inventions of enthusiastic dreamers, or of visionaries with poetic gifts.

Authentic witness can be found among all peoples of the earth. In every age there lived a few who consciously experienced life "beyond" and brought mankind objective testimony from the realm of Spirit.

The garment worn by such communications may have been cut to suit the fashion of its day. Also it may show the colors of the Faith which at the time was held to be the *only* truth. Yet one who probes beneath the surface will everywhere and underneath each veil behold the very same, the *human self,* and that eternal *self's* profoundest self-experience: its conscious *oneness* with the wellspring of all Being in the dimensions of Eternity, and also all Existence through every sphere in space and time.

Once the reader has begun to understand what the ascent that I am tracing for him in my books demands that *he* accomplish—and to which heights even those who show but little aptitude are capable of rising, already in this present life—he will no longer ask me: "What am I to do?" and then, ignoring everything I wrote, expect me to disclose some esoteric "exercise."

For he will then have comprehended that his goal is something infinitely more sublime than seeking wondrous fakir powers; infinitely more sublime than all the most inexplicable tricks of occultism; and infinitely more sublime than any "secret" doctrine of a sect that worships mental fictions and drapes its fantasies in pseudoscientific motley.

In order to be understood, at least by those who are the most in danger, I am compelled to speak in images with which such readers are familiar. Sometimes, too, in Eastern terminology such as it nowadays is common knowledge, thanks to theosophical literature. But one who goes a little deeper shall soon discover that the source of which I write has in the past been heard of only in distorted form.

Even a professional orientalist who is familiar with every text of Eastern wisdom ever published, and currently accessible, will find in them no more than hidden references to the source of which I speak. Because the sacred writings of antiquity were only for the eyes of those who had already heard, by word of mouth, what is the essence of these secret texts.

The authors of the ancient sacred writings had purposely combined dry records, chronicles, and narratives—in which no trace of any secret insights are contained—with their authentic knowledge, which was to be intelligible only to prepared initiates. Indeed, the surface meaning of their texts will frequently convey the very opposite of what was understood by minds who were informed.

BESIDES, THE FACTS PRESENTED in my books were only seldom written down, even in such cryptic form, and even then only in fragments.

The manuscripts, however, in which these fragments have been gathered will never be accessible, today or in the future, to uninformed outsiders. And everyone is here considered "uninformed" who has not yet, in spiritual ways, *experienced* in himself what might be called the "canon" of the insights set down in these texts, as knowledge that remains attainable to human spiritual perception.

THE FEW WHO PERMANENTLY live this kind of knowledge, and who are, therefore, also able to convey it, have very carefully respected, until most recent times, certain ancient laws that categorically forbade the public presentation of even such few hints as I am now obliged to give.

Only when the rigorous interpretation of these laws gave way to a more lenient view did it become permissible to state this knowledge openly, as in the present book. This was not possible before the highest powers in the Spirit's hierarchies—whose lowest members are a few incarnate mortals here on earth— had sanctioned this more lenient view as needed in the interest of many at this time.

If one would fully grasp what here is stated publicly, one has to clear one's mind of any notion that what I bring is merely still another shade of some religious creed, or propaganda for an Eastern system of philosophy.

A reader who will seek in records of historic times for traces of the insights here discussed will certainly discover them.

In purest form such knowledge was alive in people of antiquity, during the archaic age of ancient mystery religions.

To practiced ears, however, every age will clearly speak of it in its own way and language. Nor is it difficult to notice that the timeless fountainhead from which the present witness stems was widely influential on this planet even until recent times as the perennial source of inspiration for every human group or body whose loftiest ideal had been—or may be still—to help man find his highest inner goal.

Much more could still be said in this connection, but here it cannot be discussed. For these are matters to be found by those alone for whom they are intended.

A PERSON WHO WOULD REAP the fruits that grow inside the garden where such knowledge is enclosed will have to make all of his earthly life one never ending exercise.

The new life that he means to find is even now contained within his present everyday. He only has not yet discovered it.

And so he has no need to turn to mystagogues purveying "secret teachings," only to be given "exercises" causing grievous harm; because his ordinary daily life is, in the end, the most effective, *truly spiritual* "exercise" he could desire. And it is one that the Eternal Light itself has given him to practice, in order that he may perfect himself thereby each day anew.

In his ordinary daily life, in the most natural and simple form—without all mystifying humbug—he then shall, at the proper time, achieve the highest level of perfection that he is able to attain in life on earth. He shall not find perfection in some esoteric school, nor in the wake of counterfeit initiates who have the front to pose as spiritual "guides"—individuals for whom one can but ask forgiveness, because they know not what they do.

The way that leads to spiritual perfection demands the human being as a whole.

Body and *soul* are not to be experienced separately if one would reach man's highest goal in *fact*.

There is nothing in man's earthly body that is merely "physical"; nothing that is not at once connected with his soul. Nor is the task one should pursue to "spiritualize" the mortal body, but rather to "incorporate" the Spirit's life, by virtue of the soul's dynamic elements. It is a task one can accomplish here on earth, and its results are then experienced in this mortal life.

Those who treat the earthly body with contempt, yet even so would find the timeless realm of Spirit, whose very substance is eternal light, will land instead within another circle of delusions.

What *is* demanded of the mortal organism, however, is that it learn to sense, and to have faith in, the nonphysical, *eternal* self that lives concealed within it, and for whose life it shall become a tool and vessel.

Begotten by the Spirit, man's timeless self contains the wellspring of all his spiritual energies. His mortal organism, on the other hand, provides him with a tool: a vessel he can sink into that inner well to raise the Spirit's energies into his conscious physical existence.

In this eternal *self* we find our timeless nature: conscious as eternal beings born within Eternity.

Only in this inmost *self* can we attain the radiant Spirit's all-embracing substance.

Only in the innermost of your own *self*—the self eternally begetting who you are—shall you receive your timeless *Living God*.

NOT INTELLECT NOR WEALTH OF learning may attain the highest goal that man is able to achieve in life on earth.

Spiritual perfection is the result of life and living. It is not a mere abstraction carved by razor-sharp intelligence.

Much there is, indeed, that only mental effort can bestow. Such knowledge ought one to acquire—through the mind—in order to possess it.

But then the sage will rise above all mental knowledge, until he learns to think as children think.

It is not *childish* thinking that you are to learn, but rather to experience—once again—that state in which both thinking self and object thought are *one*.

It was in such identity that, as a child, you formed the very first thoughts in your mortal mind. And only in the like identity can one conceive the very highest *thoughts*.

When, as an infant, you began to *think,* your mind did not itself produce the content of your thinking, but rather found it given in your earliest surroundings and experience. Similarly, your *spiritual* experience must, in the end, supply you the material with which you afterwards may build the dome that is to crown the temple of your knowledge.

Then, however, you have not lived your earthly life in vain, nor borne its pain and sorrows to no purpose.

Securely rooted in your present life, you may in confidence look forward to your life "beyond"—this very day assured of your eternal being in the Spirit's everlasting realm of light.

REMINDER

"Yet here I must point out again that if one would derive the fullest benefit from studying the books I wrote to show the way into the Spirit, one has to read them in the original; even if this should require learning German.

"Translations can at best provide assistance in helping readers gradually perceive, even through the spirit of a different language, what I convey with the resources of my mother tongue."

From "Answers to Everyone" (1933), *Gleanings*. Bern: Kobersche Verlagsbuchhandlung, 1990

By the same author:

The Book on the Living God

Contents: Word of Guidance. "The Tabernacle of God is with Men." The "Mahatmas" of Theosophy. Meta-Physical Experiences. The Inner Journey. The En-Sof. On Seeking God. On Leading an Active Life. On "Holy Men" and "Sinners." The Hidden Side of Nature. The Secret Temple. Karma. War and Peace. The Unity among Religions. The Will to Find Eternal Light. Mankind's Higher Faculties of Knowing. On Death. On the Spirit's Radiant Substance. The Path toward Perfection. On Everlasting Life. The Spirit's Light Dwells in the East. Faith, Talismans, and Images of God. The Inner Force in Words. A Call from Himavat. Giving Thanks. Epilogue.

The Kober Press, 1991. 333 pages, paperback. ISBN 0-915034-03-4

This work is the central volume of the author's *Enclosed Garden*, a cycle of thirty-two books that let the reader gain a clear conception of the structure, laws, and nature of eternal life, and its reflections here on earth. The present work sheds light on the profound distinction between the various ideas and images of "God" that human faith has molded through the ages—as objects for external worship—and the eternal *spiritual reality*, which human souls are able to experience, even in this present life. How readers may attain this highest of all earthly goals; what they must do, and what avoid; and how their mortal life can be transformed into an integrated part of their eternal being, are topics fully treated in these pages.

What sets this author's works on spiritual life apart from other writings on the subject is their objective clarity, which rests upon direct perception of eternal life and its effects on human life on earth. Such perception is only possible, as he points out, if the observer's *spiritual* senses are as thoroughly developed to perceive realities of timeless life, as earthly senses need to be in order to experience *physical* existence. Given that authentic insights gathered in this way have always been extremely rare, they rank among the most important writings of their time, conveying knowledge of enduring worth that otherwise would not become accessible.

The Book on Human Nature

Contents: Introduction. The Mystery Enshrouding Male and Female. The Path of the Female. The Path of the Male. Marriage. Children. The Human Being of the Age to Come. Epilogue. A Final Word.

The Kober Press, 2000, 168 pages, paperback, ISBN 0-915034-07-7

Together with *The Book on the Living God* and *The Book on Life Beyond*, *The Book on Human Nature* forms a trilogy containing guidelines toward a new and more objective understanding of both physical and spiritual realities, and of the human being's origin and place within these two dimensions of creation.

The Book on Human Nature at the outset shows the need to draw a clear distinction between the timeless spiritual component present in each mortal human, and the material creature body in which the spiritual essence is embodied during mortal life. The former, indestructible and timeless, owing to its being born of spiritual substance, represents the truly human element in what is known as mortal man. The latter, physical, contingent, and subject to decay and death, is no more than the temporary instrument the spiritual being uses to express itself in physical existence. Given that the spiritual and animal components within human nature manifest inherently discordant aspects of reality, they typically contend for domination of the total individual. Experience shows that in this conflict the animal component with its ruthless drives and instincts clearly proves the stronger.

To help the reader gain a realistic understanding of the

human being's spiritual and physical beginnings, by way of concepts more in keeping with humanity's advances in every discipline of natural science, the book explains, to the extent that metaphysical events can be conveyed through language, the timeless origin and source of every human's spiritual descent. It likewise shows that the material organism, now considered mankind's primal ancestor, existed long before it was to serve the spiritual individuation as its earthly tool. In this context the author points out that the traditional creation story, such as it has survived, is not simply an archaic myth, invented at a time that lacked the benefits of modern knowledge, but instead preserves, in lucid images and symbols, a truthful view of actual events. Events, however, that did not happen merely once, at the beginning of creation, but are a process that continues even now, and will recur until this planet can no longer nurture human life.

Even so, the principal intention of the present work, as well as of the author's other expositions of reality, is not so much to offer readers a new, reliable cosmology, but rather to encourage them to rediscover and awaken the spiritual nature in themselves, and thus to live their present and their future life as fully conscious, truly human beings.

The Book on Happiness

Contents: Prelude. Creating Happiness as Moral Duty. "I" and "You". Love. Wealth and Poverty. Money. Optimism. Conclusion.

The Kober Press, 1994. 127 pages, paperback. ISBN 0-915034-04-2.

Sages and philosophers in every age and culture have speculated on the nature, roots, and attributes of happiness, and many theories have sought to analyze this enigmatic subject. In modern times, psychology has joined the search for concrete answers with its own investigations, which frequently arrive at findings that support established views. Still, the real essence of true happiness remains an unsolved riddle.

In contrast to traditional approaches, associating happiness with physical events, the present book points to the spiritual source from which all human happiness derives, both in life on earth and in the life to come. Without awareness of this nonmaterial fundament, one's understanding of true happiness is bound to be deficient.

The author shows that real happiness is neither owing to blind chance, nor a capricious gift of luck, but rather the creation of determined human will. It is an inner state that must be fostered day by day; for real happiness, as it is here defined, is "the contentment that creative human will enjoys in its creation." How that state may be created and sustained, in every aspect of this life, the reader can discover in this book.

The Book on Solace

Contents: On Grief and Finding Solace. Lessons One Can Learn from Grief. On Follies to Avoid. On the Comforting Virtue of Work. On Solace in Bereavement.

The Kober Press, 1996. ISBN 0-915034-05-0.

In this book the author shows how sorrow, pain, and grief, although inevitable burdens of this present life, can and ought to be confronted and confined within the narrow borders of necessity. Considered from the spiritual perspective, all suffering experienced on this earth is the inexorable consequence of mankind's having willfully abandoned its given state of harmony within the Spirit, a deed that also ruined the perfection of material nature. Although the sum of grief thus brought upon this planet is immense, human beings needlessly expand and heighten its ferocity by foolishly regarding grief as something noble and refined, if not, indeed, a token of God's "grace."

Understanding pain objectively, as a defect confined to physical existence, which, even in exceptional cases, is but an interlude in every mortal's timeless life, allows the reader to perceive its burdens in a clearer light, and thus more patiently to bear it with resolve.

While suffering, through human fault, remains the tragic fate of physical creation, the highest source of solace, which helps the human soul endure its pain and sorrow, continually sends its comfort from the Spirit's world to all who seek it in themselves. How readers may discover and draw solace from that inner source the present book will show them.

The Wisdom of St. John

Contents: Introduction. The Master's Image. The Luminary's Mortal Life. The Aftermath. The Missive. The Authentic Doctrine. The Paraclete. Conclusion.

The Kober Press, 1975. 92 pages, clothbound. ISBN 0-915034-01-8.

This exposition of the Fourth Gospel is not a scholarly analysis discussing the perplexing riddles of this ancient text. It is, instead, a nondogmatic reconstruction of the actual events recorded in that work, whose author wanted to present the truth about the Master's life and teachings; for the image propagated by the missionaries of the new religion often was in conflict with the facts. The present book restores the context of essential portions of the unknown author's secret missive, which the first redactors had corrupted, so that its contents would support the other gospels.

Written by a follower of John, the "beloved disciple," its purpose was to disavow the "miracles" the other records had ascribed to the admired teacher. His record also is unique in that it has preserved the substance of some letters by the Master's hand, addressed to that favorite pupil. Those writings are reflected in the great discourses which set this gospel text apart and lend it its distinctive tone.

Given the historic impact of the man presented in this work, an accurate conception of his life and message will not only benefit believers of the faith established in his name, but also may explain to others what his death in fact accomplished for mankind.

The Meaning of this Life

Contents: A Call to the Lost. The Iniquity of the Fathers. The Highest Goal. The "Evil" Individual. Summons from the World of Light. The Benefits of Silence. Truth and Verities. Conclusion.

The Kober Press, 1998, paperback. ISBN 0-915034-06-9.

This book addresses the most common questions people tend to ask at times when circumstances in their daily lives awaken their awareness of the many unsolved riddles that surround the human being here on earth. To be sure, philosophy and teachings of religion have offered answers to such questions through the ages, but as these often draw on speculation, or require blind belief, they can no longer truly satisfy the searching mind of our time.

It is against this background that the present book will guide its readers to a firmer ground of understanding, resting on objective insights and experience. From this solid vantage, readers may survey their own existence and its purpose with assurance.

As this book explains, the key to comprehending the meaning of this present life is, first, the insight that this life is but the consequence of causes in the Spirit's world and, thus, has of itself no meaning other than that fact. And, secondly, the recognition that material life is ultimately meaningless if human beings fail to give it meaning: by virtue of pursuing goals whose blessings shall endure. The nature of the highest goal that mortals can pursue provides the substance also of the present book.

About My Books, Concerning My Name, and Other Texts

Contents: Frontispiece portrait of the author. Translator's Foreword. About My Books. Concerning My Name. In My Own Behalf. Important Difference. Résumé. Comments on the Cycle *Hortus Conclusus* and the Related Works. The Works of Bô Yin Râ. Brief Biography of Bô Yin Râ.

The Kober Press, 1977. 73 pages, paperback. ISBN 0-915034-00-X.

This book presents selections from the author's works that let the reader gain a clear conception, both of the spiritual background and perspective of his writings, and of their extraordinary range and depth. For readers seeking knowledgeable guidance through the labyrinth of speculations, dogmas, and beliefs concerning *final things*, his expositions will provide a source of comfort and enduring light.

And since, from the "perspective of eternity," human beings bear responsibility to practice spiritual discernment, lest they be deceived by falsehoods, readers here will find reliable criteria to clarify their own beliefs regarding mysteries that neither mental powers nor religious faith have ever fully answered.

By showing that objective knowledge of spiritual existence is not only possible, but that attaining such experience is finally the foremost task of human life, these books become essential guides for readers seeking inner certainty, which mere belief cannot create. In this respect it is the practical advice these books provide which is their most remarkable characteristic.

Spirit and Form

Contents: The Question. Outer World and Inner Life. At Home and at Work. Forming One's Joy. Forming One's Grief. The Art of Living Mortal Life.

The Kober Press, 2000.

The underlying lesson of this book is that all life in the domain of spiritual reality, from the highest to the lowest spheres, reveals itself as lucid order, form, and structure. Spirit, the all-sustaining radiant *substance* of creation, is in itself the final source and pattern of all perfect form throughout its infinite dimensions. Nothing, therefore, can exist within, or find admittance to, the Spirit's inner worlds that is devoid of the perfection, harmony, and structure necessarily prevailing in these spheres.

Given that this present life is meant to serve the human being as an effective preparation for regaining the experience of spiritual reality, this life must needs be lived in ways that are consistent with the principles that govern spiritual reality; in other words, ought to be lived according to the structure, laws, and inner forms of that reality. To show the reader how this present life receives enduring form, which then is able to survive this mortal state, the book sheds light on crucial aspects of this physical existence and advises how these may be formed to serve one's spiritual pursuits.

Worlds of Spirit
A Sequence of Cosmic Perspectives

Contents: Preface. The Ascent. The Return. Reviews of Creation. Epilogue.

Illustrations: *Emanation. In Principio erat Verbum. Lux in Tenebris. Te Deum Laudamus. Space and Time. Primal Generation. Seeds of Future Worlds. Emerging Worlds. Birth of the External Cosmos. Labyrinth. Desire for External Form. Astral Luminescence. Sodom. Inferno. De Profundis. Revelation. Illumination. Fulfillment. Victory. Himavat.*

The Kober Press, 2001. Xxx pages, hardcover. ISBN

If all the books of Bô Yin Râ, objectively considered, are unparalleled in the extensive literature on subjects touching final things—in that their author did not publish speculations based on faith or thought, but gave the reader fact-based insights into spiritual reality—the volume *Worlds of Spirit* occupies a special place even among these thirty-two unprecedented works; for in this book he integrated twenty reproductions of his paintings, representing *spiritual perspectives*, to illustrate selected aspects of his text.

While the works of the *Hortus Conclusus* cycle constitute the first authentic, comprehensive exposition of metaphysical realities, the paintings in this volume represent, in turn, the first objective visual renditions of spiritual dimensions in their dynamic figurations, colors, and inherent structure. Together with the written word—the book describes events experienced and perceived by an awakened human spirit—the images are meant to offer readers lucid concepts of nonphysical existence, and thereby to assist them in developing their own perceptive faculties.

In Preparation

BÔ YIN RÂ
An Introduction to His Works

Contents: Preface. About My Books. Concerning My Name. In My Own Behalf. Comments on the Cycle Hortus Conclusus and the Related Works. Catalogue of The Works of Bô Yin Râ. Essential Distinction. Résumé. Brief Biography of Bô Yin Râ.

Perception
60

MMD
63

Time | Space
73

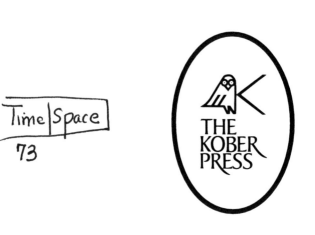

THE
KOBER
PRESS

TO DIE
19- means (Sleep)
    20-21
28 no pain
31) Last connections
35 GUIDES - (40)
61 / 41

SPIRIT
23- Workers
41- Worlds
43 - LOVE
52- In Spirit
Awakened
54
67 LIVE In Spirit
68

Pain
30
32 Cremation

Phantom Worlds
25/37
34 ABSOLUTE
   REALITY

54-55

SPIRIT
Temple of
ETERNITY
(70) Spirit's (71)
   World
(73)
75- Food / Drink

LIVING
47-48

CPSIA information can be obtained at www.ICGtesting.com
Printed in the USA
BVOW04s0210310314
349272BV00001B/2/A